W9-CKL-918

100
GREATEST
FOOTBALL
HEROES BY MAC DAVIS

GROSSET & DUNLAP
Publishers • New York

About the Author

Mac Davis has been widely known as a storyteller. Readers of his twenty previous sports books number in the millions. But many more sport fans have heard his fascinating stories broadcast over hundreds of radio and television stations throughout the United States, Canada, and even in Europe. Over the years, he has created and written many of the most popular sport shows ever presented on the air, hosted by some of the most famous sportscasters in America.

Other Sports Books by Mac Davis

100 GREATEST SPORTS HEROES	BASEBALL'S UNFORGETTABLES
100 GREATEST SPORTS FEATS	FOOTBALL'S UNFORGETTABLES
THE GIANT BOOK OF SPORTS	PACEMAKERS OF SPORTS
TEEN-AGE BASEBALL LEGENDS	SPORTS SHORTS — AMAZING,
GREAT SPORTS HUMOR	STRANGE BUT TRUE

THE GREATEST IN BASEBALL

1974 PRINTING

LIBRARY OF CONGRESS CATALOG CARD NUMBER: 73-822

ISBN: 0-448-11533-0 (TRADE EDITION)
ISBN: 0-448-03932-X (LIBRARY EDITION)

COPYRIGHT © 1973 BY MAC DAVIS.
ALL RIGHTS RESERVED UNDER INTERNATIONAL
AND PAN-AMERICAN COPYRIGHT CONVENTIONS.
PUBLISHED SIMULTANEOUSLY IN CANADA.
PRINTED IN THE UNITED STATES OF AMERICA.

Contents

	Page		Page
Jim Thorpe	9	Wilbur ("Pete") Henry	93
Johnny Unitas	12	Yelberton Abraham Tittle	95
Walter Camp	15	Emlen Tunnell	97
Knute Rockne	17	Elmer Kenneth Strong	99
George Gipp	19	Gale Sayers	101
Sammy Baugh	22	George Halas	103
Pat O'Dea	25	Raymond Berry	106
Frederick ("Fritz") Pollard	27	Benny Friedman	107
Harold ("Red") Grange	29	Bobby Layne	109
Amos Alonzo Stagg	31	Charley Trippi	111
William ("Pudge") Heffelfinger	33	Steve Van Buren	113
Otto Graham	35	Vince Lombardi	115
Bronko Nagurski	38	Bill Dudley	118
Frank Hinkey	40	Earl ("Dutch") Clark	119
Ernie Nevers	42	Frank Leahy	120
Sid Luckman	44	Charley Brickley	121
Larry Kelley	46	Willie Heston	122
Jimmy Brown	48	Clarke Hinkle	123
George Blanda	51	Roy ("Link") Lyman	124
Doc Blanchard and Glenn Davis	53	Earl ("Curly") Lambeau	125
Don Hutson	55	George McAfee	126
The Four Horsemen	57	Guy Chamberlin	127
Byron ("Whizzer") White	60	Danny Fortmann	128
John Victor McNally	62	Clyde Turner	129
Glenn Scobey ("Pop") Warner	64	Walt Kiesling	130
Joseph Napoleon Guyon	67	Paul Brown	131
Marion Motley	69	Cliff Battles	132
Mel Hein	70	Richard Marvin Butkus	134
Joseph Willie Namath	72	George Trafton	136
Chuck Bednarik	75	John William Heisman	137
Cal Hubbard	77	The Heisman Memorial Trophy Winners	139
Elroy Hirsch	79	The 10 All-Time Winningest College Football Coaches	140
Eddie LeBaron	81	The 10 All-Time Winningest Professional Football Coaches	140
Lou Groza	84		
Paul Leroy Robeson	86		
Jerry Kramer	88		
Bob Waterfield	91		

Foreword

On November 6, 1869, in a cow pasture at New Brunswick, New Jersey, a team from Rutgers University tangled with a team from nearby Princeton College in the first intercollegiate football game ever played in America. It was the beginning of all competitive football play in the United States.

Since that historic day, countless men have sought fame and glory in gridiron competition, and many have been acclaimed as football heroes. To tell the stories of all the fabulous players of this game would fill innumerable volumes. In this book only one-hundred have been chosen, but their gridiron achievements encompass the whole glorious history of America's favorite sport. There never were more memorable football heroes than these.

Through the pages of this book march the fantastic players and coaches, the trailblazers of the game, the pacemakers, the innovators, the record setters, and all other greats who made and shaped football history from the beginning to the present day.

This book will take fans of all ages on an exciting, fascinating journey through more than a century of glorious years, and to an intimate meeting with the most magnificent heroes the game of football ever had.

100 Greatest Football Heroes is an invitation to all football buffs for a most rewarding reading adventure.

Mac Davis

JIM THORPE
Superman Was an Indian

You, sir, are the greatest athlete in the world!''

The awe-struck King Gustav of Sweden said it emotionally to a 24-year-old American Indian one summer day at the 1912 Olympic Games in Stockholm.

Performing as a one-man track team, Jim Thorpe had swept to victory in fifteen different track-and-field events to become the first and only man in Olympic history ever to win both the decathlon and pentathlon.

James Francis Thorpe was more than just the greatest athlete in the world by royal acclamation, however. An incredibly skilled performer in a dozen different sports, he was famed also as the greatest all-around athlete America ever had.

Humbly and unnoticed, the fantastic saga of Jim Thorpe began in 1888, when, as a twin, he was born in a one-room cabin at Prague, Oklahoma, to an Indian mother and a half-breed father. *Wa-Tho-Huck* was his Sac-Fox tribal name, meaning Bright Path, and bright indeed was his path to immortality as the greatest football player there ever was.

He first became identified with football at the age of eighteen when he left the reservation to enroll as a student in the United States Indian Industrial Institute at Carlisle, Pennsylvania, also known as Carlisle College. That little school for Indians fielded a football team for intercollegiate competition.

At Carlisle, Jim Thorpe became the most versatile and most magnificent all-purpose halfback ever seen in college football. Blessed with an indestructible physique, awesome strength, and matchless stamina, that bushy-haired, 6-foot-2-inch, 185-pound Sac-Fox Indian did everything ever achieved by man in gridiron warfare. He was a triple-threat football player beyond compare.

Always playing effortlessly, he ran with blinding speed and remarkable elusiveness. He tackled and blocked harder than any man who ever played the game. In the early years of the forward pass, no one was his equal at pitching footballs. He had no peer as a broken-field runner. In every game, with spectacular long runs, he would score at least two or three touchdowns. No enemy defense could stop Indian Jim when he was on the gridiron warpath.

Added to all his incomparable gridiron skills, he was as phenomenal a kicker as ever lived. He was supreme in punts, placements, or drop-kicking. It was not unusual for him to kick several 50-yard field goals in a game. He kicked booming punts for 80-yard distances, and at times he even zoomed punts the entire length of the field, 100-yarders.

In his heyday, Jim Thorpe performed all sorts of miracles for college football

history. Once, in a game against a mighty, undefeated, championship West Point team, he caught the opening kickoff and ran 95 yards to a touchdown. But when that play was nullified by the referee, and Army again kicked off, Indian Jim again caught the ball and this time raced 100 yards for a touchdown!

Another time, when Harvard ruled the collegiate football world, he demolished the championship Crimson team single-handedly by drop-kicking four field goals from fifty to seventy yards in length and scoring all the points for the Carlisle team. It was one of the most unforgettable upsets in football history.

Jim Thorpe raced across the stage of big-time college football, leaving in his wake the most surprised, bewildered, battered, and beaten teams in American football. He spearheaded his Carlisle teammates to stunning upset victories over the football champions of the nation — East, West, North and South. Whenever yardage or a touchdown was needed, Jim Thorpe would often growl at his teammates in a Carlisle huddle, "Give me the ball and stay out of my way!" And, more often than not, he would be off for a touchdown. He was impervious to injury, playing 60 minutes of every game.

His gridiron exploits with the Carlisle Indians not only won him every collegiate honor there was to win, but also made him a living legend.

Jim Thorpe's final two seasons in college competition were the most glorious ever achieved by any one player. In seven of the nine games Carlisle won in 1911, Thorpe ripped loose for touchdown runs of 85 yards or more, while scoring from twenty to thirty points a game. In 1912, his last hurrah in college play, American football was almost one-hundred percent Jim Thorpe. He had led Carlisle to twelve victories in fourteen games against the most powerful teams in the country. He had been on the loose for 25 touchdowns, booted 38 field goals, and scored a record 198 points.

Ironically, that fabulous year of football glory was Jim Thorpe's sad farewell to amateur athletic fame, for when the Amateur Athletic Union questioned his purity as a true amateur athlete, Jim Thorpe turned from college football to big-league professional baseball. He became a major-league outfielder and starred in the big leagues for eight years.

But his heart and love were still for football. So, in 1915, at age 27, he joined the Canton Bulldogs of Ohio, where pro football began. As their player-coach he not only revived the fading fortunes of that once-prominent pro football team, but also of big-time professional football itself. Football fans flocked in large numbers to see wondrous Indian Jim run again for touchdowns and kick incredible field goals. Jim Thorpe was pro football's most glamorous and greatest star for sixteen years.

When his fabulous glory years as football's greatest player ran out, it was all downhill for the legendary Indian. He wound up in poverty, neglected and humiliated by a fickle sports world which once had worshipped him as the most wondrous athlete of all time.

On March 28, 1953, Jim Thorpe was found lifeless on the floor of his shabby trailer in Oklahoma. His courageous heart had given out. His body was brought back to Pennsylvania, where he had made imperishable college football history as the greatest of all All-America heroes, and placed in a 20-ton marble mausoleum built high on a ledge in Flagstaff Mountain Park, in the town of Mauch Chunk. And that town changed its name, henceforth to be identified as Jim Thorpe, Pennsylvania.

Indian Jim Thorpe became the first football player to be twice immortalized for his gridiron exploits, for he is now enshrined in the College Football Hall of Fame, as well as the Pro Football Hall of Fame. But his last and most glorious hurrah came in the midst of the 20th century, when all the sports historians unanimously voted him the ultimate greatest football player of all time. So Jim Thorpe will remain down through the ages — the greatest footballer of all.

JOHNNY UNITAS
The Unwanted Quarterback

The most inspiring rags-to-riches story in all football history was the Cinderella saga created by John Constantine Unitas.

Although once unloved and rejected as a football player, he nevertheless became the most extraordinary and most magnificent quarterback that football has known. There never was another gridiron hero in history with the total quarterback skills of Johnny Unitas.

Born on May 7, 1933, in Pittsburgh, Pennsylvania, a child of poverty, Johnny grew up to be a skinny 145-pound quarterback for St. Justin High School. Surprisingly, he distinguished himself as a schoolboy quarterback by being chosen for the All-Catholic High School team of Pittsburgh. When he was ready for college, though, he was dismayed to discover that no college wanted him as a football player. Not one college had offered him an athletic scholarship. Since his widowed mother could not afford to pay his college tuition, unhappy Johnny was resigned to go to work.

But just when it seemed that obscurity would swallow him, he was invited to a football tryout at the University of Louisville. Skinny Johnny so impressed the college football coach there with his quarterbacking skills and determination that he was offered an athletic scholarship.

In the four years that followed, Unitas beefed himself up to 190 pounds, stretched over a 6-foot-1-inch frame, and became one of the South's finest college quarterbacks. Upon graduation, he happily found himself to be a ninth-round draft choice by his hometown big-league pro team, the Pittsburgh Steelers of the National Football League.

All too soon, Johnny Unitas again experienced the heartbreak and disappointment of being an unwanted quarterback. In training camp, the Pittsburgh Steelers quickly cut him from their football squad, and advised him to go home and forget about ever becoming a big-time pro football player. No other team in the National Football League wanted him, so, broke and miserable, Johnny hitchhiked home, a failure even before his pro football career had begun.

In that heartbreaking year of 1955, twenty-three-year-old Johnny Unitas, already burdened with the responsibility of a wife and child, loved football so much and so firmly believed in his own ability that, while toiling as a pikedriver, he still found the time and energy to play semi-pro football with a sandlot team known as the Bloomfield Rams for six dollars a game.

Then came a lucky day in the following year when he was spotted by a scout for the Baltimore Colts, then a bedraggled winless team of the National Football League. It was a club in dire need of a good quarterback at a cheap price. The Colts acquired Johnny Unitas for exactly eighty cents — the cost of a long-distance phone call from Baltimore to Pittsburgh.

There wasn't much fanfare to herald Johnny's arrival as the Baltimore Colts' quarterback. His debut in the big-league pro ranks was a travesty and a disaster. As he first raced onto the field to play in a scheduled game against the Cleveland Browns, he tripped and fell flat on his face before he even reached the huddle. The first time he threw a forward pass, it was intercepted and resulted in a touchdown for the rival team. The next pass from his center he fumbled, and the ball was scooped up for another touchdown by the rival team. Then followed another bad pass by Unitas, and another fumble, until his first pro game ended in a rout for his team. Final score: Colts 27, Cleveland Browns 56.

From that humiliating beginning, a legend began to grow. Johnny Unitas was not discouraged. He was still filled with iron-willed determination to succeed as a quarterback. Fortunately for football history, his first major-league coach (Wes Eubank) was patient, sympathetic and understanding enough to keep rookie Unitas on his team. Johnny came back in the games that followed. Before his first pro season ended, he was being acclaimed as a superior quarterback.

As the football seasons passed, Johnny Unitas grew into more than the greatest quarterback of his time. He grew into a living legend, putting together the most consistent and greatest show of forward

passing ever seen in football. Before he began to weave his gridiron legend, there may have been quarterback ball-handlers with more deceit and dexterity, greater passers, smarter play-callers, and tougher competitors in grid-battle, but never was there a quarterback great with the total skills of Johnny U. He did it all.

For seventeen years, he quarterbacked the Baltimore Colts with fantastic accomplishments. He compiled an avalanche of records for his fame, and he changed the once humble and winless Colts into an awesome football power — a veritable football dynasty. Again and again, quarterback Unitas masterminded and paced the Colts to National Football League titles and world football championships.

Johnny Unitas was beyond compare for the most incredible gridiron performances imaginable. In the final moments of a game, when it came to racing the clock for an impossible victory, he was supreme in daring and deadly efficiency. Unitas, the Colts, and victory became synonymous.

The greatest forward-passing feats in the National Football League practically began and ended with Johnny U. Like throwing more complete passes for more yardage and more scores than any other player in football history. Only he ever gained 300 or more yards in a single game, passing — 23 times. He also threw touchdown passes in 47 consecu-

tive games — one football record that may remain unchallenged forever.

In some 200 games, he threw more than 4,000 forward passes, completing more than half of them, to gain more than 40,000 yards — about 35 miles of gridiron ground! He rushed for more than 2,000 yards, and his amazing passes produced more than 300 touchdowns.

No wonder Johnny Unitas became as powerful a crowd-magnet as ever starred in football, the first quarterback in history to command a season's salary of $100,000!

Even when he was forty years old, and had nothing more to gain for his fame in accolades or affluence, his love for football combat was still so fierce that he continued playing in major-league football, as a quarterback of class and glamour, still respected and feared by the opposition as no other forward passer ever was.

Neither time nor any fantastic accomplishments of other great quarterbacks will ever impair or diminish the glorious legend of Johnny Unitas. Always he will shine as an inspiration in football's history books, and wherever and whenever boys will dream about winning fame as quarterbacks, their dreams will be enriched by the example of what Johnny Unitas did to become perhaps the greatest of all quarterback immortals.

WALTER CAMP
The Father of Football

The game of football has changed amazingly in many ways since Walter Chauncey Camp named his first All-America team in 1889. The canvas jacket and the flowing locks have long since disappeared. The eastern Big Three — Harvard, Yale, and Princeton — no longer dominate the college game; there is no dominance by any section of the country. And while there were only a few enthusiasts watching games in Camp's day, the grid game — high school, college, and professional — now draws more than 50,000,000 spectators annually, and as many more are television viewers.

If it had not been for the innovations brought into the game by Walter Camp, football might never have grown into the gigantic spectacle it is today. Indeed, Camp merits his recognized acclaim as the Father of American Football.

He was born in 1859, the son of a New Britain, Connecticut, high school principal, and grew up in New Haven in the shadow of the elms of Yale University. He was small and slight as a boy, and his bearing wasn't much more impressive athletically when he entered Yale in 1876. But by the time he was graduated four years later, his determination to excel in everything had won him a reputation as a prominent athlete. He was a member of

every varsity team then in existence at Yale. He was halfback and captain of the football team, a track star, a pitcher in baseball, a great swimmer, a stroke on the rowing team, and he played tennis.

A few years after being graduated, Camp returned to Yale as football coach, an unpaid job in those days. The game played then had little resemblance to the game played today. It was a kind of combination Rugby, soccer, and American football, and there were no permanent rules. Some games were played with twenty-five men on a side, others with fifteen.

Camp loved the game with a passion, and he set out to formalize it and give it a standard format. His ideas were revolutionary. First, he established a complete set of rules. He established the official number of players at eleven on a side. He invented the scrimmage method of putting the ball in play. He developed team signals, used guards as interference on end runs, and originated the snapback from center. He instilled in his players this key idea: Keep your eye on the ball. And he introduced the idea of four downs to gain ten yards, truly the keystone of modern-day football. He also handed down the scoring system for touchdowns and field goals.

As champion of the game he loved so

tion. He did this in 1889 when he selected the first All-America team. His football terrain, however, was limited to the teams he personally saw in action, and thus his first twenty-two All-America nominations were all from Harvard, Yale, or Princeton. Several University of Pennsylvania performers edged into the sacred circle after a few years, but it was not until 1898 that a player from the Midwest — Herschberger of Chicago — made the select list. It was not until 1918 that a Southern college merited a pick — Ashel Day of Georgia Tech. And it was not until 1921 that Brick Muller of California brought All-America fame to the West Coast.

Nevertheless, Camp's selection of a "dream team" of college players kindled national attention in the game. It became the ambition of every college player to be named to the Walter Camp team. Although imitators sprang up everywhere, the highest honor for thirty-six years was to be selected by Camp, who continued to make his selections until the time of his death in 1925. After that, there continued to be a Walter Camp All-America list every year, but it was picked by football writers, officials, and coaches from every section of the country, thereby giving it a national flavor to match the spread of grid talent across the nation.

Camp wrote more than thirty books on football and physical fitness.

Football today has developed into a different kind of game from that envisioned by Camp. But football today stands in his debt. For he laid the cornerstone and directed the erection of the superstructure. Every football stadium now filled with a colorful, cheering crowd is a memorial to the Father of Football.

passionately, Camp led the fight to save it when some college officials frowned on it as a waste of time. The changes he wrought made football less a bloody brawl between two massive groups of giants and more the scientific, precise, skillful exhibition it is today.

Perhaps his outstanding contribution was the naming each year of the best players in the country, one at each posi-

KNUTE ROCKNE
"The Bald Eagle Flew High"

On the morning of March 31, 1931, when an airplane suddenly tumbled from the skies into a Kansas cornfield, that shocking tragedy snuffed out the life of a bald, flat-nosed, 43-year-old football figure known the world over as Knute Rockne. He was the most fabled, most colorful, most glamorous, most dynamic, and most vibrant coach in the history of college football. Strange was the road he had traveled to become a legend in his lifetime.

Knute Rockne was born in 1888, in the town of Voass, Norway, the son of a carriage maker. Brought to the United States when a boy, he grew up in the poverty of Chicago, Illinois. He became a high school dropout to work as an obscure clerk in the post office. Nevertheless, he educated himself, and in 1910 he came to the famed University of Notre Dame at South Bend, Indiana, even though he was neither an Irishman nor a Catholic. Prematurely bald, broken-nosed, the 22-year-old undergraduate looked like a teenaged old man. If at that time anyone had dared predict that this unlikely candidate would ever achieve a reputation as the most vibrant figure in college football history, the laughter would have split the heavens.

Yet, this was exactly what Knute Rockne did. He became Notre Dame's first famous football player. As a fleet-footed and clever end with an amazing talent for catching forward passes, then seldom used in grid warfare, Rockne not only won headlines for himself, but actually brought about a new era in game strategy.

When his playing days were over, Knute Rockne tried to lose himself in the obscurity of teaching college chemistry. But the "Golden Age of Sports" was beginning to flower, and Knute Rockne was persuaded to become head football coach of Notre Dame.

He became more than just another college football coach. He became so ingenious and famous as a coaching wizard that he actually grew into an American institution. He fathered modern football by turning a college boys' game into big business, with multimillion-dollar stadiums for football games played before crowds of 100,000 spectators at each gridiron battle. More than any man in history, Rockne "sold" college football and made it a game for the masses. He became the brain, the heart, and the soul of modern high-geared football.

At Notre Dame he built a football dynasty, developing and molding winning football teams which became the greatest of their time in intercollegiate competition. He brought an extra dimen-

sion to college football. His razzle-dazzle, swift-striking football teams, featuring exciting wide-open play, changed it from a dull, rough, brutal game of beef, muscle and power into a game of speed, daring strategy, astonishing skills, color, suspense, surprise and thrilling drama.

Notre Dame football teams became wonder-elevens of perfection in timing, sharpness and execution. The Fighting Irish roamed all over the gridiron map, playing against the outstanding college teams in the nation, and they rarely tasted defeat. In the thirteen seasons of Rockne's reign as a football coach, Notre Dame went through five seasons undefeated, and each time they wound up acclaimed as the undisputed national college football champions.

In those thirteen glorious years, Rockne piloted his Fighting Irish to 105 victories and only 12 losses.

"The Bald Eagle," as Knute Rockne came to be described throughout the football world, was a genius as a college coach. His hold on his players was complete, because he was truly fond of them as human beings, and always interested himself in their private lives. A clever psychologist, his half-time locker-room pep talks were legendary. He infused his teams with a spirit of pride and confidence to achieve remarkable victories.

Moreover, he was an exceptional teacher of football. His lessons stayed with his young pupils for life. He not only produced more All-America stars for gridiron glory than any other college football coach, but many of his Notre Dame players became outstanding and successful football coaches in their own right — an astonishing total of eighty-nine.

At the peak of his glory, coach Rockne's fame rivaled that of United States presidents. Hollywood produced motion pictures of his life and career, books were written about him, an automobile was named after him, and people sang songs about "The Rock of Notre Dame."

When Rockne perished in the plane crash, an entire nation was stunned, and millions wept for the coach who had taken Notre Dame to unparalleled football heights. They came from all walks of life, and from all over the world, for his funeral. The services were broadcast to every corner of the world.

A guard of honor, composed of the foremost Notre Dame players, carried him to his grave. He was buried in the shadow of the Notre Dame campus, and his monument under a huge tree is now a shrine.

Knute Rockne has been gone for many years now, but time will never dim his legend as the king of college football coaches. In 1969, when intercollegiate football commemorated the one-hundredth anniversary of its birth, a panel of football historians, experts, and the game's most famous coaches, participating in a centennial poll, reached back across the years and bestowed a unique honor upon Knute Rockne. He was acknowledged as the greatest coach in the first 100 years of college football.

GEORGE GIPP
"One for the Gipper"

George Gipp was the first famous football player in history to give his life for the game.

He died at the peak of his college gridiron glory, at the tender age of twenty-three, and so revered a legend was he by then that his ghostly spirit continued to prevail in collegiate football play and win games for his team long after his tragic death.

Born in 1897, in the mining town of Laurium, Michigan, the son of a minister, Gipp was a strange hero for football immortality. An exceptional all-around high school athlete, he came to the University of Notre Dame on a baseball, basketball,

and track scholarship. He had no love for the game of football, nor little inclination to play it.

Nevertheless, one afternoon the Notre Dame football coach Knute Rockne chanced to see George Gipp, on the campus for the first time, amusing himself by kicking a football. Although he was wearing street shoes, the newcomer was drop-kicking the football for more than sixty-five yards in distance. Coach Rockne lost no time in persuading Gipp to come out for the football team.

Thus began the fabulous legend of "The Gipper of Notre Dame." His first varsity football season was cut short by a broken leg. The following season, Gipp dropped out of school to enter military service in the first World War. But he returned in 1919 to become quickly Notre Dame's most glamorous and greatest football hero.

The exploits of that lean 175-pound six-footer in college-gridiron warfare established him as a football miracle man. No player of his time could buck a line, knife a tackle, toss a forward pass, or hip-weave his way through a broken field for spectacular touchdown runs better than "the Gipper." Moreover, whenever he punted a football, it was not unusual for him to drop-kick a 65-yard field goal.

With his astonishing speed of foot, his bewitching elusiveness, his quick and daring thinking in a clutch, he sparked the Fighting Irish to many magnificent victories over the most powerful college teams in the nation. Once, in a single

game, he ran for 332 yards. The Gipper's incredible gridiron feats became legendary.

Curiously, while George Gipp was making imperishable college football history as Notre Dame's most glamorous football player, he took his fame lightly. His zest for adventurous living and pursuit of wild excitement off the field involved him in so many questionable escapades that he almost was expelled from school. But coach Rockne always came to Gipp's rescue and saved him for greater glory. The Gipper repaid Rockne's loyalty and understanding with wondrous gridiron feats which produced a host of victories for Notre Dame.

Gipp's final game in college football came on a bitter cold and snowy November afternoon in 1920 against an undefeated Northwestern University team. When the contest began, fabulous Gipp was resting on the bench, suffering with a heavy cold. He had suited up, despite his coach's advice, just to be ready to play if called upon. But coach Rockne had no intention of playing him that day.

As the game went into its final minutes of play, though, with Notre Dame needing a touchdown score for a victory, the frenzied crowd in the packed stands began to chant a wild call for the Gipper's appearance on the playing field. The irrepressible Gipper pleaded with his coach to play only a few minutes in his farewell to Notre Dame glory. Most reluctantly, Rockne sent the Gipper into the game, just for a few plays. And with one of his spectacular broken-field runs, he scored the winning touchdown for his team. It was the Gipper's last heroic feat.

Only a few hours later he was in a hospital fighting for his life. He had come down with a streptococcal throat infection and pneumonia. As that fabulous All-American fullback lay dying, the entire Notre Dame student body, 1,500 strong, knelt in the snow outside the Gipper's hospital room, praying for his recovery. And in churches across the nation, football fans from all walks of life added their prayers for George Gipp. But it was all in vain. With coach Knute Rockne at his bedside, the Gipper died in the flower of his youth. And a legend was born.

A glorious football winner in life, the tragic Gipper remained a football winner even in death, because for years thereafter Knute Rockne was to invoke his memory to win many games for Notre Dame. "Win one for the Gipper" became an inspirational battle cry. At times, when an imminent defeat faced a Notre Dame football team, coach Rockne would gather his players around him for an emotional locker-room pep talk.

"Men," he would say, "I was with Gipp at the end before he died in my arms. His last words to me were, 'Coach, sometime when the team is up against it, and when things are going wrong, and the breaks are beating the boys, ask them to win one for the Gipper!'"

Almost always, an emotion-stirred Notre Dame football team, fired up by the spirit of George Gipp, scored impossible victories to win "one for the Gipper!"

For years after his early death, the legendary Gipper exercised such a weird and unbelievable spiritual influence on Notre Dame football teams that he helped the Fighting Irish to many victories by being their ghostly "twelfth man" in the lineup.

The immortal George Gipp was the only gridiron great who ever won football games for his college team alive and dead!

SAMMY BAUGH
Slingin' Sam, the Passin' Man

Once upon a time, in the not so long ago, there came out of Texas an ambitious boy hunting for football fame. Before he was done with his quest for gridiron glory, he had created such an unparalleled legend as a forward-pass wizard that he will be remembered forever as "Slingin' Sam, the Passin' Man."

He left behind him so many incredible passing records that quarterbacks are still shooting at them. He revolutionized the forward pass to such a high art form that forward passers are still measured by the standards he set both as a college and professional football player.

Born on March 17, 1914, near Temple, Texas, Samuel Adrian Baugh, the son of a railroad worker, began to pay football when he was only ten. As he grew older, lanky and frail, he barely made the Sweetwater High School football team as a quarterback. He was so determined to improve his accuracy as a forward passer that he practiced in secret. He hung an old automobile tire from two ropes fastened to the branch of a tree, and he had his brother push it so that it swung like a pendulum. Sammy Baugh became so proficient slinging a football that he could take off on a dead run, cock his arm, and still fire a pass through the middle of the swinging tire. With his accurate forward passing, Sammy almost twice piloted his only-average high school team to the state championship.

Following his humble schoolboy gridiron glories, Sammy Baugh came to Texas Christian University, then little-known. He really wanted to make the baseball team, but when the baseball coach, also then the freshman football coach, saw Sammy fling a forward pass, he convinced him to play football, too.

Baugh developed slowly as a college football quarterback. He made no headlines until he was in his junior varsity year, but then suddenly he blossomed out, and he actually turned the whole approach to college football play completely around. Before, the forward pass was rarely used by college quarterbacks, and mostly on a third down, or when a game seemed hopelessly lost. The ingenious and daring Sammy Baugh, directing the offense of the "Horned Frogs," now passed on first down, passed on fourth down, passed from deep in his own territory, and even passed from two feet out. His daring aerial bombardment changed the strategy in intercollegiate football warfare.

"Slingin' Sam," as they dubbed him, not only pitched Texas Christian University to many victories, but his matchless forward passing led TCU to Rose Bowl and Cotton Bowl triumphs, as well as a national football championship. He left

TCU not only with a multitude of All-America honors, but also hailed and acclaimed as the most valuable college player in the history of the Southwest Football Conference.

After his college years of gridiron glory, "Slingin' Sam" came to big-league professional football. As a rookie, he signed with the Washington Redskins of the National Football League for a modest salary of only $8,000 a season. He was a fantastic bargain.

In 1937, when he made his professional debut, he was an immediate sensation. He astonished and dazzled a crowd of more than 85,000 spectators at that game by throwing sixteen spectacular passes and completing eleven. The five he didn't

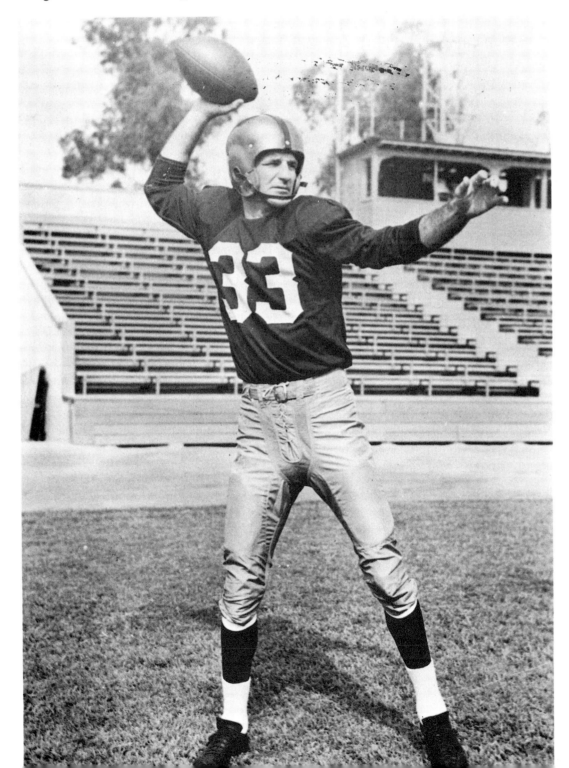

complete, though perfectly thrown, were dropped by his clumsy receivers.

From his first season in the violent world of big-time pro football, "Slingin' Sam, the passin' man" (as he came to be widely known and feared in awed admiration) established himself as one of the most magnificent backs pro football had ever seen. With his fantastic forward passing, he also revolutionized professional football. When he first came on the scene, the forward pass was an outcast piece of wild and useless strategy. It was a weapon rarely used, mainly in desperation. But "Slingin' Sam" threw forward passes so often, and with such daring success, that the forward pass soon became accepted by every major-league football team as an offensive staple and dangerous gridiron weapon for victory.

As the Redskins' fabulous quarterback, Sammy Baugh made up his own plays on the spur of the moment. In his initial season with the pros, he gained more than a thousand yards with his forward passes. One season, he completed 111 of 117 attempted forward passes.

The incomparable forward pass was only one of Sammy Baugh's grid-weapons for his fame as one of football's greatest players. He was a superb punter who at times booted the ball in games for 85 yards. Some of his kicking records still stand. He was equally good on defense as well as offense. He could run with astonishing speed, and he was sure-handed and deadly as a safetyman.

Surprisingly, despite his seemingly frail body, he was amazingly durable. He was a 60-minute player in most games, and during his National Football League career, stretching over sixteen seasons, Sammy Baugh played in every game. It is said that he wore out more than 60 pairs of football shoes, 30 pairs of pants, at least 100 jerseys, and ten helmets.

"Slingin' Sam," because of his forward-passing wizardry, became the meal ticket for the Washington Redskins team. Tremendous crowds flocked to see how he performed his magic for all professional football.

In Baugh's first ten years with the Redskins, that team did not have a single losing season. Five times he quarterbacked them to their division title, and twice his forward passes took them to football's most glorious heights, the National Football League crown and the world championship.

He was a most unusual gridiron-god. Always modest, a perfect gentleman, he never drank, and always lived by the clock. Though he was the most glamorous and greatest forward passer of all, surprisingly, he was rewarded poorly for his incomparable exploits on the gridiron. His penurious club owner never paid him more than $15,000 a season.

In 1952, after sixteen fabulous years of glory, he finally retired from professional football as a player. He left behind him an unbelievable record of greatness as the most efficient forward passer of all time. Out of 3,016 attempts, he completed an amazing 1,709 forward passes for a total of 22,085 yards and 187 touchdowns.

Twice Sammy Baugh was crowned for posterity as a football immortal. He was one of the first college football players to enter the National Football Hall of Fame. And, in 1962, when the National Professional Football Hall of Fame opened as a shrine for its immortals, Sammy Baugh was among the first players to enter that hallowed pantheon.

In football history, the fantastic legend of "Slingin' Sam, the passin' man" will stand out like a beacon light for all great forward passers to see and marvel at.

PAT O'DEA
The Vanishing Wonder

Patrick John O'Dea, football's earliest kicking star, was something of a man of mystery. It is known that he was born in Australia late in the last century, that when he came to the United States to enroll at the University of Wisconsin he had never even seen an American-type football game, and that after gaining incredible stardom he disappeared from sight for seventeen years until a sportswriter found him hiding and living under an assumed name.

But halfback Pat O'Dea's kicking mastery had no mystery about it. He was without a doubt the greatest drop-kicker and placement-kicker the world ever knew. He could curve a punted football the way a baseball pitcher curves his throws. He could punt 85 yards consistently. He once drop-kicked on the dead run and split the uprights fifty yards away. Another time he was cornered by defenders around midfield, sidestepped them neatly, and kicked another score. In those days, if a team kicked the ball over the goal line, the rival team had to kick off in return from its own 25-yard line. Then, if a fair catch was called for, the original team could drop-kick or place-kick for a score. That was the system used by Wisconsin during O'Dea's four-year reign there. Under ordinary conditions, punts of 70 and 80 yards were the rule with him, and often he punted 100 yards. No wonder he was hailed as "the greatest kicker of all time"!

O'Dea had been an outstanding amateur athlete in Australia in his youth.

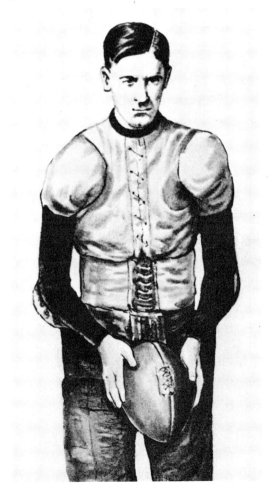

Australian football in those days was more polite than the American game. With little body contact, it was more like a punting contest than the grid game that was developing in the United States. But O'Dea made the transition smoothly when he arrived at the Wisconsin campus at Madison. As soon as his coach saw the distance he could kick a ball (and with accuracy!), O'Dea was a first-stringer.

In one of the first night games ever played, Wisconsin played Pop Warner's Carlisle Indians in 1896. It was Pat O'Dea's first game, and it was scoreless until the third period. Then O'Dea punted 50 yards, high over the light standards, and the ball landed close to the Indian goal line. A Wisconsin end fell on it and rolled over the goal, which in those days was a legitimate touchdown. The Carlisle players hadn't even seen the play, so high was Pat's kick out of the range of the lights. Throughout his career, O'Dea could kick as high or as low as his ends, rushing downfield, desired. His kicks had the accuracy of a long forward pass.

There were many highlights in his career. Once, against Northwestern, a heavily favored opponent, O'Dea so impressed the Wildcats with a 63-yard drop-kick (still the world's record) that they floundered into a 48-0 defeat. Against Beloit, another tough opponent, O'Dea kicked four field goals and returned a kickoff 90 yards for a touchdown. Against Minnesota, O'Dea, trying to evade opposing defenders, found himself cornered, but managed to drop-kick on the dead run, resulting in a 40-yard scorer that started a 39-0 rout for Wisconsin.

Although not a big man (6 feet, 170 pounds), he had extraordinary strength. Once, in a tight spot, the little Wisconsin halfback had the ball and was trying to score, but ran into a mob of enemy tacklers. O'Dea read the situation, picked up the scatback, ball and all, and plunged over the goal line. There apparently was nothing O'Dea couldn't do well. He became the Wisconsin Badgers' first All-America football star.

Naturally, he was a marked man in every game he played. It was rare when he did not play the full sixty minutes. Because of his fantastic, superhuman kicking, he became a football legend in his lifetime. And the legends grew after his glorious college playing days were over.

He settled in San Francisco to work as a lawyer, but his fabulous football fame as the greatest kicker of all time turned his private life into shambles. Wherever he went and whatever he did, mobs of frenzied admirers besieged him. To escape from his football fame, Pat O'Dea changed his name to Charles Mitchell and vanished into total obscurity. No one knew what had become of Pat O'Dea. Even his brother believed that Pat had returned to Australia where he had quietly joined the Australian Army and had been killed in action in the First World War.

But seventeen years later, an inquisitive reporter discovered that the unknown Charles Mitchell was truly the once-famous football hero, Pat O'Dea. With his secret finally revealed, he resumed life under his real name, explaining his long and strange disappearance to the wondering public: "I just didn't want to be Pat O'Dea, the big football hero, any longer."

Nevertheless, in the record books the name of Pat O'Dea will always be inscribed with the other immortals of football history. He was a pacemaker for kicking glory beyond compare.

FREDERICK ("FRITZ") POLLARD
The Black Pioneer

Every football season, hundreds of black players throughout the United States work, sweat and quest for gridiron glory on countless college teams and the big-time professional football teams, where only the best in the game can perform. Over the years, many Negroes have become superstars of the game for their imperishable fame. Most black football players, past and present, may not know it, but all owe a debt of gratitude to "Fritz" Pollard, the first Negro to achieve national fame as a college football hero and in professional football when there were virtually no other blacks playing football anywhere.

Pollard was the first black in college football history to achieve All-America honors. He was the first black to play in the glamorous annual Rose Bowl classic. He was the first Negro to play in organized professional football. And, moreover, he was the first black to coach a professional football team composed mainly of white players.

Though Fritz Pollard was only five feet, six inches in height and weighed but 155 pounds, he became a legend at Brown University in Providence, Rhode Island. Once, on successive Saturdays, he almost singlehandedly defeated Yale and Harvard when those Ivy strongholds were the most important and most powerful collegiate teams.

It was an epic feat at that time, especially for a black player. Diminutive Fritz paced the Brown team to many other historic victories against the best football teams in the nation. Despite his size, Pollard was a versatile and magical player. He rushed, passed and ran back punts in a manner never before seen in the Ivy League. He was like a brilliant comet streaking across a college gridiron, as one historian of that time said publicly.

In 1916, Walter Camp named Pollard on his annual All-America team, designating him as the best college halfback in the nation. Despite his color, there were few prejudiced football fans who disputed the choice. It has been said that there never was a better or more spectacular performer on the football field, inch for inch, pound for pound, than the tiny black wonder from Brown University.

Born Frederick Pollard in Rogers Park, Illinois, a suburb of Chicago, in 1894, he was the son of a former slave. The father had come out of the South shortly after the Civil War to join the Northern Army stationed in Kansas. The older Pollard became a boxing champion of the armed forces. He had three sons and four daughters. The men in the family all became prominent athletes. But little Fritz achieved the greatest game of all. He was a star baseball player at Brown, and also set many track records as a hurdler.

After college, Fritz Pollard became head football coach at Lincoln University in Pennsylvania for several years, and then was a backfield coach at Northwestern University.

Then he became head coach of a professional team! It was a historic "football first" for a black man. He directed the Akron (Ohio) Indians, a club which won the world's professional football crown in 1920. The players were mostly white and it was a challenge for Pollard, particularly since he had to direct Southern whites. But Pollard, as player-coach, earned their respect with his scintillating performances on the field.

Pollard took his team to the West Coast for nine games against college all-star teams — and won them all.

Later, Fritz played for other pro clubs, including the Milwaukee Badgers and the Hammond Pros, and he finished his grid career with the Providence (Rhode Island) Steamrollers. As player-coach of the latter club, he once played against the immortal Red Grange in an exhibition game, and he amazed an overflow crowd of 50,000 fans by outshining the legendary "Galloping Ghost" while sparking and piloting the Steamrollers to a 9-6 victory.

In a football era which presented more obstacles to black players than open doors to gridiron fame and fortune, Fritz Pollard performed incredible feats as a football player, college and pro. His greatness as a pioneer, to show the way for all other black players who were to follow him to gridiron fame, will never be forgotten.

HAROLD ("RED") GRANGE
The Galloping Ghost

The fabled Golden Age of Sports, back in the 1920's, was the stage for many never-to-be-forgotten immortal sport champions, such as Babe Ruth in baseball, Jack Dempsey in boxing, Paavo Nurmi in track, Bobby Jones in golf, and Bill Tilden in tennis. But none of the big names of that golden era surpassed the name of Red Grange, the most glamorous college football player in history. In his three playing years at the University of Illinois, he captured the imagination of the public as no other football player ever had. He became a household word.

A gifted broken-field runner, Red Grange wreaked havoc on the best college teams in the land, and recorded the most fabulous minutes in college football. He dodged, weaved, twisted, glided and bucked for touchdowns as no other football player ever had. He was so elusive, as he flitted through, around and over the finest players of the game, that he became nationally known as "The Galloping Ghost." He also blocked, tackled, passed, punted, and kicked placements. More than a million people flocked to football stadiums to see him perform his gridiron miracles.

He was born on June 13, 1903, in Forksville, Pennsylvania. His mother died when he was five and his father, a lumber-camp foreman and one-time police chief, moved the family to Wheaton, Illinois. Red was an outstanding athlete at Wheaton High, with an incredible record as an all-around sports performer. He won sixteen varsity letters in football, basketball, baseball, and track.

When he came to the University of Illinois, because it was the cheapest place for a college student without an athletic scholarship, Grange was reluctant to go out for football. He stood only five-feet-ten, weighed only 170 pounds, and thought that the huge members of the football squad would bury him. But at the insistence of his fraternity brothers, who wanted a gridiron hero among them for prestige, he tried out for the team — and not only made it, but also became the superstar of American football.

One Saturday, for instance, against the powerful undefeated Michigan Wolverines, Grange took the opening kickoff on his 5-yard line and started up field. He started to the left, reversed his field to avoid one man, and then, cutting across the field, ran diagonally through the oncoming Michigan players. At the Michigan 40-yard line he was in the open and he scored standing up on a 95-yard run that dazzled the 67,000 fans. It was a scene that was to be repeated throughout Grange's college and professional career.

After three glittering collegiate football seasons (31 touchdowns, 4,280 yards gained from scrimmage, and three-time All-America), the famed redhead turned professional and became pro football's first $100,000-a-year player. When he made his pro debut with the Chicago Bears of the National Football League on Thanksgiving Day, 1925, he caused the wildest mob scene in football history. More than 100,000 people turned out to see him play, although the Chicago ball park could seat less than half that number.

The lure of Red Grange's magic football prowess was unbelievable, because until then, pro football had been in low standing with the public. It attracted little attention on the sports pages, and few paying customers. But with his glamorous fame and unmatched prestige, Red Grange almost overnight gave new life to big-time pro football, and started it off on the glory road to its present state of national popularity and affluence.

Grange starred in professional football for ten years, and his exploits as a gridiron marvel did not go unrewarded. He earned more than a million dollars. The whole world came to know about him when Hollywood made a film of his life and football career. He had become a legend in his lifetime.

He is now immortalized both in the College Football Hall of Fame, as well as the Pro Football Hall of Fame. No other player before him had enriched college and pro football with such glamour, drama, color, prestige, and matchless thrills as the "Galloping Ghost."

AMOS ALONZO STAGG
The Longest Journey to Glory

The list of original contributions to football made by Amos Alonzo Stagg is incredibly long. His influence is seen in every phase of the modern game. Many a present-day coach, after "inventing" a gimmick for offense or defense, has learned that Stagg, the Grand Old Man of Football, used it thirty or forty years earlier.

Stagg, who lived to be 103 years old before his death in 1965, is the only man immortalized in football's Hall of Fame both as a player and as a coach. In all, he was a football coach for an unbelievable span of seventy years. On mileage alone, he rates as the number one coach of all time.

Born in West Orange, New Jersey, in 1862, son of a poor shoemaker, Stagg in his youth planned to be a minister. As a divinity student at Yale, he was persuaded to play baseball and football. He excelled in both. As an end in football, he was selected in 1889 by Walter Camp for the first All-America team ever named. After he left Yale, Stagg became football coach at an obscure YMCA training school known as Springfield College. His devotion to clean play and Christian ideals sprang from his early pulpit ambitions, and in the seven decades of his football successes that were to follow he never wavered from those standards.

In 1892, when the University of Chicago opened its doors, Amos Alonzo Stagg became its football coach. He stayed there for forty-one years, and throughout that period he became known as the most inventive of coaches.

Stagg invented the tackling dummy. He was the first coach to use the spiral pass from center, the first to use multiple and fake ball handling, the first to use the unbalanced line, the first to use a huddle, the first to use a fake place kick, and the first Midwestern coach to use the forward pass, adding to it variations of his own, such as a double delayed pass and a double pass with a forward pass. He was the first coach to number football players, and the first to organize an intersectional game between college football teams.

And his teams were a success. Some of

his unbeaten elevens were among the greatest in the history of college football. At Chicago, he coached nineteen Western Conference championship teams, won 254 games, lost 104, and tied 28. He developed many All-America gridders who became football immortals.

In 1933, when he reached the age of seventy, the University of Chicago gratefully made him a professor emeritus and retired him on a $3,000-a-year pension. But the proud old coach turned down the pension, saying, "I could not and would not accept a job without work. I am fit, able and willing to continue as a football coach. I refuse to be idle and a nuisance."

So he went west and became football coach at the tiny College of the Pacific where for fourteen more football seasons he coached his teams to fifty-nine victories, seventy-seven defeats, and seven ties. It was a remarkable record because the small college, always with a skimpy football squad, played against the biggest and most powerful football teams in college competition.

At the age of eighty-one, white-haired coach Stagg came up with such a wonder winning football team that he was voted by all the college football coaches in the land to be "the best college football coach of the year."

In 1947, the College of the Pacific tried to retire Stagg as its football coach and make him a "consultant," but again he turned down the honor, saying as he had before that he would not accept a job that involved no work. He went east and joined his son, Alonzo, who was football coach at little Susquehanna College in Pennsylvania. There, for six more years, the Grand Old Man of Football went on the field daily for vigorous coaching of offense. And because of his valuable

coaching, the Susquehanna football team recorded an undefeated season in 1951.

What his players remember most about Stagg's dedication was his devotion to clean play. Stagg beamed his pep talks toward team pride. He specifically refrained from building resentment against the opposing team. Above all, Amos Alonzo Stagg kept football in its place. He never viewed the game as an end in itself.

He didn't mollycoddle his men, either. He kept after them with a sharp tongue. So the chastened men who played under him learned more than how to hand off a football. Once, when asked what it was like to be a coach, Stagg replied:

"To me, the coaching profession is one of the noblest and most far-reaching in building manhood. No man is too good to be the athletic coach for youth. Not to drink, not to gamble, not to smoke, not to swear . . . to be fair-minded . . . to deal justly . . . to be honest in thinking and square in dealing . . . not to bear personal malice or to harbor hatred against rivals . . . not to be swell-headed in victory or over-alibi in defeat . . . to be the sportsman and gentleman at all times . . . these should be the ideals of the coach."

They were the ideals the Grand Old Man of Football lived up to all the days of his long years. And when the end finally came, this amazing man who had quit coaching after seventy consecutive years, at the ripe age of ninety-eight, could look back over his football travels with pride. His football journey was the longest and most glorious ever taken by a coach. It had produced more victories than ever achieved by any other football coach in history — 314.

It was a coaching record for the ages.

WILLIAM ("PUDGE") HEFFELFINGER
First of the Professionals

In the rugged pioneering days of football, and for a very long time after, the name of Pudge Heffelfinger was spoken with reverent awe by football followers. During the early days of gridiron competition, Pudge, who weighed only 205 pounds in his prime, was perhaps the toughest, roughest, and most durable player who ever stepped on a football field.

Pudge was a three-time All-America star at Yale University, and he was the father of many football "firsts," including the play in which a guard pulls out to lead interference. Actually, he played competitive football over a fifty-year period, the last time when he was nearing his sixty-sixth birthday.

According to the records in the Professional Football Hall of Fame, he was the first player in history ever to be paid a substantial amount of money for a grid game. That was in Canton, Ohio, in 1892, three years before the first professional football team was organized. For playing in a game between two Pittsburgh athletic clubs, lineman Pudge, as the first true pro gridder, was paid $500.

As a pacemaker, Heffelfinger broke a lot of ground in other areas, too. Born William Walter Heffelfinger on December 20, 1867, the scion of a wealthy and socially prominent family in Minneapolis, young Pudge was drawn to the football field early in life. Eligibility rules were extremely lax in those early days of football, so at the same time he was starring for his high-school team, he was permitted occasionally to play with the University of Minnesota football team. As soon as he graduated from high school, he headed straight for Yale and football glory.

When he arrived at New Haven, Pudge had hopes of becoming a back, as he had been in high school. But Yale's famous playing coach, William ("Pa") Corbin, told him that the team needed linemen more than backs, and he ordered him to play guard. It was a momentous decision that would shape Yale football history. In the four years that Pudge was a roving guard, he spread fear and havoc among Yale's grid opponents. He paced and sparked his teammates to astonishing exploits. In the 1888 season, with Pudge crashing through enemy lines, leading the interference, and with his lightning-like rushes into enemy backfields, the Yale team rolled up a staggering 694 points. And not a single point was scored all that season against the Blue Line, protected by fierce Pudge Heffelfinger and his inspired teammates. In the four seasons he starred for Yale as guard, the Elis played fifty-seven games and won fifty-five of them. Durable Pudge played every minute of every game.

Mighty Pudge's role as a grid terror was not exclusively a defensive one. He was a powerhouse when Yale had the ball. With his immense speed and tireless energy, he was a devastating line plunger, and in runs in the open he was faster than most halfbacks. As a result, he frequently carried the ball and bowled through the opposing line. When he played the line on offense, he spearheaded the attack, smashing ahead like a tank, with the ball carrier hanging to a strap on the back of Heff's uniform. On defense, he was quick in diagnosing enemy plays. Because of his strength and speed, he could brush aside blockers and get at the ball carrier.

In his junior year at Yale, Heffelfinger evolved the idea of a guard pulling out of the line to head the interference on end sweeps. Heff mowed down would-be tacklers with a rolling shoulder block, while keeping his feet, and then moved on to nail defenders in the secondary. The maneuver introduced by Heffelfinger revolutionized end running.

Under Walter Camp, who was Yale's advisory coach, the 1891 Eli team, spearheaded by Heffelfinger, won all of its games, handily defeating Princeton and Harvard, the other members of the Big Three. Camp later maintained that this was the greatest team ever to appear anywhere, and to his dying day, he hailed Heffelfinger as the greatest guard football ever had. On virtually every all-time All-America "dream football team" chosen since, the immortal name of Pudge Heffelfinger is there as the number one guard of football.

After his college graduation, the incomparable Pudge played for a number of semipro and professional teams and was head coach, for a while, at the Universities of California, Lehigh, and Minnesota. It was while coaching the Gophers that he brought in yet another grid innovation. In those days of mass play and no forward passing, teams most often lined up on defense with nine men, shoulder to shoulder, in the line. Thus, when a hard-cracking back hit the right spot, he was likely to break through and keep on going. Pudge conceived the idea of using a seven-man line with three linebackers — making the ball carrier penetrate two lines instead of one.

When he was fifty-three, Pudge played a full sixty minutes of football against the Ohio State All-Stars in a pro game filled with famous young ex-college players. He more than held his own. "I'd have done better," he said after the game, "if I hadn't dislocated my shoulder right after the opening kickoff." Even later, when he was just short of sixty-six, Heffelfinger played in a charity benefit game at Minneapolis, and he helped his teammates, who were about a third his age, win the game.

It was not until 1954, when he was eighty-six, that death caught up with football's greatest lineman.

OTTO GRAHAM
The Era of Automatic Otto

No quarterback immortal now enshrined in the National Professional Football Hall of Fame at Canton, Ohio, for his
everlasting glory matches the unparalleled winning record created by Otto
Graham during the brief ten years he
played as a big-league pro to establish his
fame in history as the premier quarterback
of them all. In each of the ten seasons he
starred as a quarterback he inspired and
guided his team to participate in the title
game for the championship, and seven
times he pitched his team to the league
championship. It was a fantastic winning
feat for a pro quarterback, and unlikely
ever to be equaled.

The intriguing journey of Otto Everett
Graham to gridiron immortality began in
Waukegan, Illinois, where he was born
on December 6, 1921. Since both his parents were music instructors, he became an
exceptional musical youngster at an early
age. He played the piano, the cornet, the
violin, and the French horn.

But his love for music and his musical
accomplishments did not hinder him from
developing into an outstanding all-around
schoolboy athlete. At Waukegan High, he
not only was its best basketball player, but
also hailed as one of the state's greatest
hoop stars. He also won varsity letters in
baseball, football, track, and tennis.

Naturally, upon finishing high school,
a number of colleges wanted Otto Graham

as an athlete, but all the scholarship offers he received were for only his basketball skills. He chose Northwestern University, where he achieved fame as an All-America basketball player, and one of the most brilliant college hoop stars of his time.

Although football fame was of no importance to basketball hero Otto Graham, his destiny in sports history was to achieve gridiron immortality. One day, while playing some intramural football at Northwestern, his forward passing caught the eye of a football coach. Otto was persuaded to come out for the football team.

Even though his college football career began on a sour note — he tore a cartilage in his knee that required surgery — nevertheless, in the fall of 1941, he really launched his collegiate football career for glory. As a quarterback, he quickly disclosed special talents. He had a great sense of timing, imagination, daring, and an exceptional ability to throw the long pass with uncanny accuracy. It was to become his trademark for imperishable fame as a quarterback.

During his varsity football years at Northwestern, Otto's brilliance as a quarterback was obvious. He completed 156 passes in 321 attempts, for 2,162 yards. It was a Western Conference record. He won All-America honors, and was acclaimed the most valuable player in the Western Conference.

When he left Northwestern University, he joined the Naval Aviation Service. World War II was on, and pro football was far from Otto Graham's expectations for enriching his sports fame.

One day in 1945, however, Otto Graham received an unusual offer from the famous college football coach, Paul Brown. Brown had organized a new big-league professional football team, called the Cleveland Browns, to play in a newly organized football league known as the All-America Conference. Paul Brown wanted Otto Graham for his team's quarterback.

The new All-America Conference league went into operation as soon as the war ended, and in 1946 Otto Graham began his professional football career as quarterback for the Cleveland Browns. Quickly, he became the new league's premier quarterback.

In his first pro season in the All-America Conference, "Automatic Otto," as he was dubbed for his precise forward passing efficiency, completed 95 of 174 passes, with 17 of them for touchdowns. He led the Cleveland Browns to 13 out of 15 victories, plus the AAC league championship.

"Automatic Otto," with his golden arm throwing astonishing forward passes, not only earned a bucketful of records, but with his inspiring quarterbacking he became the heart of the Cleveland Browns. He made them an awesome, winning, big-league pro football team.

In his first four seasons quarterbacking for the Browns, he masterminded and pitched his team to 52 victories and only 4 losses. For four seasons in a row, his forward passes paid off with four league championships in a row. Quarterback Graham made the Cleveland Browns dominate the All-America Conference with such awesome power that the league collapsed because of lack of competition.

So, in 1950, the Cleveland Browns, though considered strictly of minor football status, were invited to join the proud and haughty National Football League, boasting of having the greatest pro football players in the world starring for its teams. Cynics scoffed at the many records "Automatic Otto" had set in the defunct AAC league, to polish his image as a truly great pro quarterback. Some skeptics believed that he would be lucky to lead the Browns to even a single victory in the tough NFL competition.

In his very first season as a quarterback in the National Football League, Otto Graham's uncanny forward passes made shambles of all NFL competition, as he pitched the Cleveland Browns to the NFL title that crowned them the pro football champions of the world. In the seasons that followed, he did it again and again, to establish his ever-growing fame as a legendary quarterback. In each of his ten years as a pro quarterback, "Automatic Otto" pitched his team into the title game, and seven times he forward-passed his team to the league championship. It was an unprecedented winning feat for a big-league pro quarterback. And he was always at his greatest in a championship title game. He set a fantastic pace for perfect quarterbacking — with records for most passes completed, most yards gained, and most touchdown passes in National Football League championship competition.

By 1954, when he was 32 years old and acknowledged to be pro football's greatest quarterback, he decided to quit. But his coach, Paul Brown, persuaded him to play one more season for his glory. Loyal to the Cleveland Browns, Otto Graham played, and again he quarterbacked and pitched his team to another world championship. All he did in that title game was throw three touchdown passes, run for three touchdowns himself, and set up two other scoring plays, to crush the powerful Detroit Lions by a score of 56-10.

Then, after playing for the Cleveland Browns for nine years, again "Automatic Otto" decided to quit the violent world of pro football. But again, his wily coach persuaded him to give one more year to football history. Graham did, and again he quarterbacked and pitched the Cleveland Browns to a world's pro football championship. Almost 100,000 saw him play his final pro game, as he gave a dazzling performance. He threw a pair of long touchdown passes, and scored two himself, to overwhelm the Los Angeles Rams by a score of 38-14, quarterbacking the Browns to their second straight pro world's football championship.

That ended for all time the fabulous Otto Graham era. He left behind him for history a fantastic and incomparable record as a winning quarterback immortal. In his brief but brilliant ten-year career as a pro quarterback he had completed 1,464 of 2,626 forward passes, for 23,584 yards and 174 touchdowns.

Even more unbelievable, in each of the ten years he played as a pro quarterback, his team participated in the title game, and seven times his forward passes won the league championship for his team.

No quarterback immortal now enshrined in the Hall of Fame ever accomplished as much for his glory in the brief time Otto Graham did. No wonder there is a belief among historians of the game that "Automatic Otto" was the greatest ever to play the quarterback position in big-league pro football.

BRONKO NAGURSKI
The Monster Who Was a Bear

Bronko Nagurski had never played football in his life until he came to the University of Minnesota, in 1926, as an eighteen-year-old, and tried out for the freshmen football team.

But before that six-foot-two 230-pound youngster was done with college gridiron glory, his name became synonymous with incredible football strength, power and greatness. He was a terrifying battering ram splintering everything in his tracks — the hardest-hitting and most devastating player ever seen in intercollegiate football competition. A sixty-minute player in every game, his ferocity on a gridiron was frightening, especially when he tore up the opposition with rampaging charges. And his versatility was amazing. In his first varsity season, he was Minnesota's greatest end. The following season, he was acclaimed an All-America tackle, and the season after, he was honored as an All-America fullback. He was the first and only college player in history ever to make the All-America team at two different positions, tackle and fullback.

Nagurski was born on November 3, 1908, to Polish-Ukranian parents who had settled in Rainy River, Ontario, some sixty miles from the town of International Falls, Minnesota. He was christened Bronislau, but when he first entered school, his immigrant mother advised the teacher, "Just call him Bronko." His nickname stayed for the rest of his life, and also became a football legend.

After Bronko Nagurski was done with college football play, he became a big-time pro with the Chicago Bears of the National Football League. Here, again, he soon became the most feared player in the game, a peerless line-busting fullback marvel who didn't need any interference to gain yardage, because he ran his own. Often, he dragged five or six tacklers with him over the goal line for a touchdown score.

As a rampaging Chicago Bear, Bronko reveled in collision, and no pro football-great before or since ever dealt out the punishment he did on a football field. A shocked and awe-struck rivel coach said it for all the football coaches and players when he once proclaimed, "The only way to stop Nagurski is to shoot him before he leaves the dressing room." Bronko was such a ferocious and awesome pro full-back that a rival club owner once actually offered him $10,000 in cash to get out of the National Football League, because he just didn't want the mighty Bronk around to ruin any more of his players. But Nagurski remained in pro football, even though his top salary as the game's greatest fullback was never more than

$5,000 a season. Curiously, off a football field, he was a gentle, soft-spoken and shy man.

While starring for the Chicago Bears, the incomparable Bronko earned extra money by wrestling professionally. He won more than 300 matches, and for a time, was even recognized as the world's heavyweight wrestling champion.

Once, he paced the Chicago Bears to a record twenty-three consecutive victories. In his time, his matchless playing sparked the Chicago Bears to world football championships. Because of him, the team became known as the "Monsters of the Midwest."

After eight glittering seasons in pro football, an attack of arthritis forced the strongest and most feared player in the game to retire from gridiron warfare. But

in 1943, after a six-year layoff, Bronko was persuaded to leave his farm and return to play for the Chicago Bears, for just one more season. Again, he paced them a world football championship. It was Nagurski's final fling of gridiron glory. He left the game with a record of 4,031 yards gained in 872 attempts — an incredible 4.7 yards for every time he carried the ball.

But the legend he left behind far exceeded mere statistics. He was established as a football immortal, and grid historians lost no time in honoring him with a place in both the college and professional Football's Hall of Fame. Bronko Nagurski as the greatest gridiron terror of all will glow in memory forever, for he remains symbolic of the ultimate in football strength and power.

FRANK HINKEY
The Tonawanda Terror

As far back as football history goes, little men have made resplendent names for themselves as gridiron heroes. Many are now in Football's Hall of Fame. The most incredible and greatest little man who ever played college football was Frank Hinkey of Tonawanda, New York.

In 1891, when he came to Yale University as an unknown freshman, he was a scrawny, frail-looking, 145-pound youngster who stood only 65 inches tall. He had a pasty face with eyes that gleamed with a strange light. Nevertheless, that cadaverous midget tried out for the Yale football team. The huge husky Yale players were all so amused at the sight of him that they completely ignored him.

But one day, a shortage of players on the scrub squad gave Frank Hinkey his chance to scrimmage against the Yale varsity team as an end, and then and there a gridiron immortal was born. The silent, somber freshman devastated all varsity interference and bowled over Yale players as if they were men of straw.

When the 1891 football season began, freshman Hinkey was not only on the Yale varsity team, but he soon became its outstanding star. Playing at end, he annihilated every attempt around his position. Cunning, tough, and game, Frank Hinkey not only solved the power of the murderous flying wedge then used in col-

lege football play, but he also wrecked more 200-pound football players than any man who ever played the game. At the end of his first football season as a college player, a coveted honor was bestowed upon freshman Hinkey. He was chosen an All-American to Walter Camp's famed annual dream team.

But that was merely the beginning of Hinkey's march to gridiron immortality. In the following three football seasons, starring for the Yale team, he played his end position as few men had done before or have done since. His uncanny ability to shadow a ball, his astonishing speed of foot, and his sheer offensive strength and defensive power has rarely been equaled. Despite his meager size and weight, he had awesome durability. In the four years he starred for Yale, he never missed a single minute of play. They nicknamed him "The Tonawanda Terror," inasmuch as tiny Frank Hinkey became the most feared college football player of his time. He led the Yale football team to victory in fifty out of fifty-one games played.

So outstanding and overwhelming was his playing that he won All-America honors four years in a row. No other college football-great has ever gained that recognition.

Silent and inscrutable, Frank Hinkey was a mystery all through his football career, even to his closest friends. Only when his glorious years were over was it discovered that he had harbored a shocking secret. During those four pulsating years at Yale University, when he was performing his fantastic gridiron feats, he was ravaged by tuberculosis.

A few brief years after he had played his last college football game, Frank Hinkey's fiery spirit burned itself out. He succumbed to the dread disease at an early age.

Now enshrined in the College Football Hall of Fame, Frank Hinkey left behind him a legend of a little man's gridiron glory that will live forever in the annals of intercollegiate football.

ERNIE NEVERS
The One-Man Football Team

Ernie Nevers, the magnificent fullback of Stanford and the professional Chicago Cardinals, came closer to being a "one-man team" than anyone who ever played the game. He could do so many things with a football on offense and so many things on defense that his incredible exploits are still talked about in awesome tones even today, decades later.

Nevers was born in Minnesota, went to high school in Superior, Wisconsin, before his family moved to California. He enrolled at Stanford University in the early Twenties and became that college's greatest athlete. He was a powerful line-plunger who ran over opponents, a first-rate blocker, tackler, passer and punter.

In his senior year he broke his left ankle in a September scrimmage and sat out most of the season. Coming in for the next-to-last game, he broke his right ankle. His coach, the famed Glenn ("Pop") Warner, devised a brace that kept Nevers on his feet. He walked through plays in scrimmage as Stanford prepared for its Rose Bowl game against Notre Dame and its legendary Four Horsemen.

Nevers played a full sixty minutes that day, carrying the ball thirty-four times, made four out of five tackles and ground out more yardage against Notre Dame's brutal famed Seven Mules than all Four Horsemen combined did against Stanford. His performance, despite Stanford's defeat, is considered the most magnificent in Rose Bowl history. As Knute Rockne said after the game, "What would that man have done to us with two good ankles? He's a fury in football boots."

He was that — and more — a bruising, untiring machine, often called a coach's dream player. His performance on the field was matched by his exemplary behavior off — faithful in training, always in prime condition, and with an unquenchable thirst for competition.

After being graduated from Stanford (which retired his "Number 1" uniform forever), Nevers went into the big-time professional ranks, in 1926, with the Duluth Eskimos. His exploits were so remarkable that the club became known as Ernie Nevers' Eskimos. In his first season as a pro, the sensational Golden Boy from California played in all twenty-nine scheduled games for his team — and of the 1,740 minutes played, Ernie missed only twenty-seven minutes, all the while churning up yardage, knocking down runners, throwing forward passes, punting and kicking goals.

In one memorable game against the New York Giants, then renowned for its matchless defensive line, Ernie carried the ball on the ground for nine straight plays on a touchdown march of fifty-five yards. In another game, he threw seventeen passes and completed all seventeen. He also once kicked five consecutive field goals, the first pro football player ever to do it.

Stricken with an appendicitis attack four days before a game with Green Bay, he came off the bench to throw a then-record 62-yard pass for a touchdown and kicked the extra point for a 7-6 victory.

Later, Nevers became player-coach of the Chicago Cardinals, the first player-coach in big-league pro history. In 1929, he set his final National Football League record. It is still unequaled.

The Cards were playing their crosstown rivals, the Chicago Bears, on Thanksgiving Day, and it was always a brutal contest. This time it promised even more fireworks, since the Bears had the immortal Red Grange in their backfield. That day, however, it was no contest between Grange and Nevers, for Ernie's performance was incredible. He not only played the full sixty minutes, but he was also all over the field, ripping the enemy line to shreds, blocking and tackling viciously, throwing deadly accurate passes, and kicking precisely.

When the final figures went up on the board, they read: CARDINALS 40, BEARS 6. And those forty points racked up by the Cards were registered by one man, Ernie Nevers, who scored six touchdowns and kicked four extra points. It was a one-game scoring record that may never be equaled in professional football.

It was almost automatic when the Pro Football Hall of Fame was instituted that Ernie Nevers, the one-man team, would be among the first players installed. He was a never-to-be-forgotten performer among the immortals of football.

SID LUCKMAN
The Kid from Brooklyn

As the first modern T-formation quarterback in professional football history, Sid Luckman played a major role in revolutionizing the game. He was a gridiron phenomenon.

Born in Brooklyn, on November 21, 1916, he first began to play football on the teeming sidewalks of New York with a ball made of rags. As he grew older, he played his scholastic football at Erasmus Hall High School, where he gained fame as the most sensational player in Brooklyn scholastic history.

Although he was swamped with tempting athletic scholarship offers from colleges throughout the United States, surprisingly he decided to seek his higher education in his home town. He enrolled in New York's Columbia University, even though there was no athletic scholarship for him there. To support himself, he worked his way through Columbia, washing dishes, running errands, and baby-sitting.

He also played football for Columbia University, and under coach Lou Little developed into one of the finest quarterbacks in collegiate football history. A glamorous triple-threat marvel who could pass, run and kick, he became a gridiron legend.

Upon his graduation from college, in 1939, the Chicago Bears of the National

Football League quickly snared Sid Luckman for pro play. Sid Luckman and the Chicago Bears were a happy gridiron marriage. With his quarterback wizardry, Luckman helped the Bears become one of pro football's greatest dynasties.

He became more than the amazing quarterback who introduced the modern T-formation to pro football. He also was a punishing blocker, an effective tackler, an unusual punter, and an excellent pass defender. He was all that in the days when great players worked a full sixty minutes of every football game played. And when it came to forward passing, Sid Luckman was at his magnificent best. He threw 50-yard passes to his receivers like a major-league catcher pegging a baseball to second base.

His twelve fabulous years with the Chicago Bears were studded with many memorable days of glory, like on November 14, 1943, in a game against a mighty New York Giants team, when he pitched seven forward passes for touchdowns — a single-game feat that has never been topped. Sid Luckman also starred in the most perfect football game ever played by one team. It was the his-

toric 1940 play-off game against the all-powerful Washington Redskins for the National Football League championship. In that never-to-be-forgotten game Luckman quarterbacked the Bears to the most devastating and unbelievable victory ever achieved in pro football history. The Bears, piloted by wizard-quarterback Sid Luckman, demolished the Redskins by a score of 73-0, the highest score ever achieved by a team in one game in all pro football history.

During his fabled pro football career, Luckman threw 1,744 forward passes and completed 964 — for 14,683 yards and 139 touchdowns. Again and again he was acclaimed the NFL's All-League quarterback, and the league's most valuable player. His forward-passing wizardry steered the Chicago Bears to five Western Division championships and four National Football League titles and world championships.

A serious shoulder injury finally forced Sid Luckman to retire from pro football play at the end of the 1950 season. By that time, so impressive was his record as a football great that he was enshrined in Pro Football's Hall of Fame as an immortal.

LARRY KELLEY
He Clowned His Way to Fame

Mention the name of Larry Kelley to an old-time football fan and he is likely to say, "Oh, yeah, he was that nutty end they had up at Yale in the thirties." It's true, Kelley was a bit of a buffoon, but he was also more than something of a football player. He made All-America, he was named the best college gridder in the country one year, and he was the only player ever to score in six consecutive Big Three games. In every Yale-Harvard and Yale-Princeton match played during Kelley's sophomore, junior, and senior years, he scored at least one touchdown.

And he was a pace-setter in bringing levity to the usual grim, clenched-teeth business of playing football.

In 1934, Princeton had a fine team and was considered a possibility for a Rose Bowl invitation, until the Yale game. A petition urging a Princeton bid was circulated just before the Yale-Princeton clash. Unfortunately for the Tigers, their back fumbled seven times in the first ten minutes. As the teams lined up after the seventh fumble, Kelley yelled at the Princeton quarterback, "Hey, Kadlic, I hope the Rose Bowl has handles on it." Another time, the Yale team was in a bus about to be driven to the Bowl for an Army game. The players were tense and choked up. Coach Pond went down the street to buy some tobacco. As he passed the bus on his return, Kelley stuck his

head out and called, "Good luck today, Ducky!" There was no more tension.

His wisecracks were duly recorded in the newspapers, and they were enjoyed by the Yale players. They admired Kelley (he was captain in his senior year) and they often passed on Kelleyisms themselves. They said that once a little player named Charley Ewart was dazed on a play. The trainer jogged out and asked the customary question to see if his head was clear: "What's your name?" Ewart looked up, winked at Larry, and said, "Kelley." Kelley yelled out, "Take him away, doc! The little nut has delusions of grandeur!"

Another time, Yale was taking a bruising from the big Quakers of the University of Pennsylvania. Finally, one Penn man said, "I thought you were a gabby guy, Kelley. A little bashful today?" "Oh,"

Kelley replied with an air of surprise, "do you fellows speak English?" (In those days Penn was notorious for recruiting big bruisers from the coal country for football duty.) In that same game, Kelley scored in a tremendous 45-yard pass play, catching the ball in the end zone as he leaped between two Penn defenders. Just then a helicopter flew over Franklin Field, trailing a red-lettered streamer that read, "Kelly for Mayor." Larry looked up and nudged a Penn man. "I wondered how long it would take 'em to find out that I was in town."

He was born Lawrence Morgan Kelley in the small town of Conneaut, Ohio. His family soon moved to Williamsport, Pennsylvania. His father, a skilled mechanic of Irish descent, had never been to college, and in those depression days it didn't seem likely that young Larry would, either. Besides, he was a shy, sensitive, bookish boy, and if there were athletic scholarships being passed out, he wasn't likely to be tapped.

But he developed physically in high school, played end on the football team, and ran the 220-hurdles in track. He worked hard at improving his grid skills, particularly at keeping his arms loose when he went out for a pass. He improved enormously, but not enough to get a football scholarship; instead, he raised his scholastic average to above ninety, and for that he was accepted at Peddie, a preparatory school in Hightstown, New Jersey. By then he weighed 180 pounds and was almost six feet tall and playing a reasonably good brand of end.

He chose to go to Yale. Kelley figured that if he were to play football, it would have to be as a pass-catching end. He made the freshman squad and played adequately when he got the chance, but there

was no indication that an All-America was in the making.

Then, as a sophomore, he began making his mark. In the opening game against Columbia he scored his first varsity touchdown on a pass from Jerry Roscoe. He had perfected a change of speeds that made him a constant offensive threat. He would pace himself at three-quarter speed as the defender raced with him, then shift into high gear and leave the enemy back in the dust. He won the Princeton game, though, with a switch of tactics. With the ball in midfield, Kelley made a spectacular catch behind his back and started for the sidelines with two Princeton men in pursuit. As he neared the line, he stopped suddenly, coming to a dead halt — and the Princeton defenders overran him and knocked each other down. Kelley strolled the final 30 yards across the undefended goal, the only score of a game in which the Tigers were 5-1 favorites.

Besides his catching prowess, Kelley was a football opportunist. On defense he was able to smell out a play, and he often made tackles on the other side of the field from his own territory. The system might not have worked for everybody, but for the carefree Kelley it paid off many a dividend.

As a junior and senior he burned up the Ivy League, making sensational catches even as he was thinking up wisecracks for the next huddle. That was the year he won the Heisman Trophy, a symbol of the outstanding college football player, became All-America, and left Yale fans with an image they've never forgotten. He may have been a kook, but he certainly knew how to become a gridiron great, setting a pace for levity and laughter in the football world that hasn't been matched by any other college player in the game.

JIMMY BROWN
The Magnificent Terror

There never was a fullback in football history more talented nor more fabulous than awesome James Nathaniel Brown, who at the peak of his gridiron fame suddenly deserted the game to embark on a new career as a motion-picture actor. His unique switch from football glory to movie fame was a drama unparalleled in the saga of football immortals.

In nine rampaging years in the violent world of big-league professional football, Jimmy Brown set incredible records that may never be topped. No gridiron hero ever ran with a football for as much yardage, and for as many touchdowns, as he did — 12,312 yards and 127 touchdowns.

Born February 17, 1936, at St. Simons Island, a tiny spot in the Atlantic Ocean just off the Georgia mainland, he had a wretched childhood. His parents separated when he was an infant, and when he was two years old, he was sent off to live with his grandmother. He never saw his father, and rarely saw his mother, until the age of seven. Then his mother brought him north to a home in Great Neck, Long Island, a New York suburb, where she toiled as a domestic maid. But even then, young Brown knew little of a real home. Often he was sent to stay with friends of the family, and often he had to sleep in different homes, on the floor, with not even a pillow to rest his head on.

He grew up footloose, and became a young tough hoodlum. Big and strong, with flashy fists, Jimmy became the leader of a juvenile gang roaming the streets of the community, ever in search of mischief and trouble.

The turning point of his aimless life came when he began to channel his restless energies into athletic activities. At Manhasset High School, he became its most versatile and greatest athlete — a star in football, baseball, basketball and track.

When Jimmy Brown was ready for college, a friendly lawyer in town persuaded him to go to Syracuse University, even though no athletic scholarship had been offered him there. The lawyer (who was a Syracuse University alumnus) arranged to pay for Brown's college tuition.

Six-foot-one-inch, 200-pound Jimmy Brown went out for the Syracuse football team. Curiously, in the beginning he was ignored by the coach as a player. Perhaps it was because he was the only black on the football squad. By the time he graduated from Syracuse, though, he had not only become that school's finest all-around athlete, an outstanding star in several sports, but he had also become as

49

great an All-American gridiron hero as ever played in college football. He gained enshrinement in the Hall of Fame, ever to be remembered as a college football immortal.

When his glorious collegiate playing days were done, Jimmy Brown came to the National Football League to play big-time pro football for the Cleveland Browns. He came to them for a modest $3,000 bonus, and a season's salary of $12,000. Oddly enough, to play pro football, Jimmy Brown had snubbed an offer of $100,000 to become a heavyweight prizefighter with the prospect of eventually challenging for the world's heavyweight championship title.

From his first season as a player in the major-league pro football ranks, Jimmy Brown became a veritable one-man gang on the gridiron. As a rookie, he led the league in rushing, gaining an incredible 982 yards. Running with elegant grace and deceptive power, he was hailed as the most explosive rushing fullback in the game. Naturally, he wound up his initial season as a pro player, honored as the "Rookie of the Year," as well as the league's All-Pro fullback.

That was only the beginning of the Jim Brown legend. In the following season, running around, over and through the most powerful enemy lines, Brown carried the ball for 1,257 yards. Thereafter, never a season passed when fullback Brown didn't rush for more than a thousand yards. He became the first football player in history ever to run for more than a mile in a single season. Only he in pro football history ever gained 237 yards

rushing in a single game — twice. He led the National Football League in rushing for eight of his nine years. It's an all-time record. During his fabulous pro career, every time Jimmy Brown ran with a football, he carried it for at least five yards, and almost every time he ran, it took several rival tacklers to bring him down to earth.

An incredible "workhorse" who never missed playing his full allotment of time in each and every game of the schedule, fullback Brown not only made the Cleveland Browns one of the outstanding football teams, but he also sparked them to the glory of world football championships. He became not only the highest-paid football player, commanding an annual salary of about $100,000, but his spectacular gridiron feats made his name a household word for greatness, and a sports hero admired by an entire nation.

In 1966, immediately after he had led his team to a championship, and he was at the height of his power and glory as pro football's greatest player, Jimmy Brown suddenly deserted the gridiron for a movie career. Again, he quickly found success, this time as a hero of fictional adventures.

So ended the football legend of Jimmy Brown, whose like as a rushing fullback may never be seen again. Although he quit playing football to become world-famous as a make-believe hero, he was a greater hero in real life, who is now enshrined in Pro Football's Hall of Fame as a gridiron immortal for the ages. The unbelievable performances he once gave for football history won't ever be matched nor forgotten.

GEORGE BLANDA
The Ageless Marvel

George Blanda, a native of Young-wood, Pennsylvania, played and starred in the violent world of big-league professional football longer than any other man in history. The incredible saga of gridiron heroics and the fantastic longevity record he created as an ageless wonder will never be surpassed nor even equaled.

Born on September 17, 1927, the son of a poor Czechoslovakian immigrant, he first gained fame as an outstanding football player at the University of Kentucky, where he was a brilliant quarterback and kicker of All-America glory. In 1949, however, when he first came to big-time pro football as a player, his welcome was frigid. The Chicago Bears of the National Football League gave that famous All-America college hero a measly bonus of $600 with the understanding that Blanda would return the money if he made the team. He did, but only as a benchwarmer, until the Bears traded him to the Baltimore Colts, who in turn quickly traded him to the Green Bay Packers, who promptly released him as an unwanted player.

Disheartened and discouraged, George Blanda was about to return home when, fortunately, the Chicago Bears rehired him. This time he remained with the Bears as a star player for almost a full decade and established himself as one of the greatest quarterbacks and kickers that ever played in the National Football League. He set a bucketful of records for

his fame. Once he kicked 156 extra points after touchdowns in a row before missing one.

At the end of the 1959 football season, when Blanda failed to persuade his club owner to pay him a larger salary than he was receiving for his versatile gridiron skills, he quit pro football playing and retired into the obscurity of the business world.

But his retirement from pro football was brief. In 1960, when the new American Football League was organized, one of its teams, the Houston Oilers, persuaded George Blanda to become their quarterback and kicking specialist.

In his first two seasons with that club, he passed and kicked the Oilers to two league championships in a row. And over the subsequent football seasons, Blanda performed astonishing feats for the history of that new pro football league. He was the first player to throw seven touchdown passes in one game. He set a record for scoring in most consecutive games (40), and he completed the most forward passes in one season (262). He kicked the longest field goal (55 yards), and he punted the most extra points after touchdowns (456). In the seven years he starred for the Houston Oilers, he dominated the American Football League with his versatile brilliance as no other player did.

Still, when George Blanda turned forty, the Oilers released him because they believed he had grown too old for the rigorous and violent conflict of big-time pro football. But brief was his unemployment as a pro football player — the Oakland Raiders promptly hired the aged veteran to be their kicking specialist and substitute quarterback. Blanda rewarded them by winning a number of games for them with his arm and toe.

In 1970, that ageless marvel surprised the entire football world by staging the most dramatic and most glorious season of gridiron heroics ever performed by a middle-aged football player. His feats of clutch forward passing and kicking bordered on the miraculous. That season, George Blanda, the oldest player in the pro game, made the "miracle finish" in football almost a common occurrence. For he won game after game for his team in the final minutes or seconds of play by throwing astonishing forward passes, or kicking incredibly long field goals of more than 50 yards in length. His "come-from-behind" clutch exploits sparked the Raiders to a league-division championship triumph.

Although in that memorable season there were 1,225 of the world's greatest football players performing gridiron heroics for the 26 teams of the National and American Football Conferences, it was George Blanda who wound up with pro football's most coveted and greatest honor. At the end of his twenty-first season in big-league pro football, at the age of 43, that incredible graybeard was acclaimed by all as "Outstanding Football Player of the Year."

In 1972, when George Blanda had completed his twenty-third season, he had not only set the most unbelievable longevity record, but he had become the outstanding record-holder and scorer in pro football. By that time, he owned at least eleven offensive all-time records, and he had been in more big-league pro football games than any other player. Moreover, he had completed almost 2,000 forward passes, had kicked an all-time record total of 288 field goals, and had become football's all-time scorer, with a fantastic total of 1,742 points.

DOC BLANCHARD and GLENN DAVIS
The Touchdown Twins

Doc Blanchard and Glenn Davis, West Point's fabulous "Touchdown Twins," were the two greatest backs a college football team ever had at one and the same time. They formed an incredible one-two offensive punch that had no equal. No running combination in collegiate history ever fired the football imagination as did Army's incomparable Touchdown Twins. They never played in a losing game. They made the Cadets of their time football's invincible team, the greatest in Army history.

Halfback Glenn Davis, a 175-pound swiftie known as "Mr. Outside," and 205-pound fullback Doc Blanchard, known as "Mr. Inside," were the brightest stars of a West Point team that may very well have been the greatest college football team in history. In a three-year period, Army demolished every opponent by overwhelming winning scores, averaging 58.9 points a game. In 1944, the peak glory-season for the Touchdown Twins, they paced the Army team to roll up an unbelievable total of 504 points.

As the one-two offensive punch of the West Point team, the Touchdown Twins scored 89 touchdowns, an average of 8.3 yards every time one of them carried the ball. So awesome were Doc Blanchard and Glenn Davis as a backfield combination that their famous coach, Earl ("Red") Blaik, often pulled them out of a

game as early as the second period, because of the compassion he had for the rival teams that were Army's grid opponents. Whenever the Touchdown Twins played, they seemed to be able to score at will.

The onslaught that Glenn Davis as "Mr. Outside" and Doc Blanchard as "Mr. Inside" launched on rival college football teams for the glory of West Point has never been paralleled. For three consecutive seasons Army was undefeated, and three years in a row wound up acclaimed as the number one football team in the nation. Blanchard and Davis were more than two amazing football players. Both were astonishingly skilled athletes. And when fate brought them together at West Point, each underlined the other's individual strength and gridiron artistry.

Glenn Davis, born a twin in 1924 in Claremont, California, was the first to arrive at West Point. He was an outstanding schoolboy athlete, winner of ten letters in all sports. When he secured an appointment to West Point, he had a glittering first season in football as an Army plebe, but, unfortunately, he flunked out as a student. Nevertheless, he returned to West Point the following year.

That's when he met his new classmate, Felix Anthony Blanchard, who had been born in Bishopville, South Carolina, the son of a once well-known college football player. Husky young Blanchard had played freshman football at the University of North Carolina before his West Point induction.

Theirs was a happy football marriage. The lighter Glenn Davis was swift as the wind, an elusive runner in an open field, an excellent passer and kicker. The heavier Doc Blanchard had bruising power, was extremely fast and shifty, a fierce blocker, and a remarkable forward-pass catcher. He also did the kicking and punting for Army. When they played together, there was no room for jealousy, for each was supremely confident of himself. Each was willing to give his all for the good of the team. Both loved the game and were fierce competitors. They were also the best of friends.

All sorts of honors were bestowed upon those two fabulous Army backs, but despite the frenzied plaudits heaped upon them in testimony of their greatness, neither ever questioned who was the more valuable player of the two. In their senior year, they were elected by their teammates as co-captains of the Army team.

When their football glory days were done at West Point, Doc Blanchard went on to become an Army career officer, and over the years he was cited for bravery in warfare, in Korea and Vietnam. Upon graduation, Glenn Davis, too, remained in the Army, but after three years he resigned his officer commission to play professional football for the Los Angeles Rams of the National Football League. Again he showed his famed fleetness and skills in pursuit of touchdowns, but after only a few seasons of pro play, a severe knee injury closed his football career forever.

Wherever football men now gather to trade memories of immortal gridiron heroes, the names of Doc Blanchard and Glenn Davis as the Touchdown Twins are still spoken in tones of awe, for they had no equal as a two-player combination in college football history. No football-pair ever enriched gridiron history with such a treasured legend as when they performed their fantastic exploits as "Mr. Inside" and "Mr. Outside."

DON HUTSON
The Man With Magic Mitts

Don Hutson was the swiftest, cagiest, and most deceptive pass-catching receiver in the history of football, and he left behind him numerous and varied records to prove that he was football's greatest end. A full page in the record book was required to list all of his incomparable exploits.

As an incredibly talented All-America end at the University of Alabama, and eleven big-league pro years with the Green Bay Packers, Hutson set records that stood unmatched for decades. In the violent world of big-time pro football, he led the National Football League in scoring no fewer than eight times. He caught 101 touchdown passes. He gained the most yards an end ever did in a lifetime — 8,010. In pass receiving he led the league eight times. And all of this brought about six world football championships for the Green Bay Packers. Nine times he made the All-Pro team, and again and again he was acclaimed the league's Most Valuable Player.

Born on January 31, 1913, in Pine Bluff, Arkansas, Don Hutson as a skinny and shy youngster showed no interest in football when he was of high-school age. But a boyhood friend who starred on the high-school team persuaded him to try out for the team. Hutson did and developed into an outstanding schoolboy player.

When he came to the University of

Alabama, though, he looked so frail as a football player that he was almost ignored by the Alabama coach. But when it was discovered that he had such blinding speed that he could run the length of a football field in 9.7 seconds, he not only made the Alabama team, but he also became the South's greatest pass receiver. He was named to the All-America team in 1932, 1933 and 1934, and in his final season in collegiate competition he paced the Crimson Tide to a national football championship and a glorious victory in the Rose Bowl.

In 1935, the slender "Alabama Antelope" who stood only an inch over six feet and weighed no more than 170 pounds came to the Green Bay Packers to play big-time pro football. Quickly he became a Green Bay hero, an incomparable end for drama, excitement and incredible exploits. That long-legged rookie outraced and outmaneuvered virtually every defenseman in the National Football League.

Astonishing was his speed of foot going downfield in pursuit of a forward pass, and unbelievable was his skill in catching forward passes. Don Hutson penetrated the most elaborate defensive alignments. Rival coaches devised all manner of defensive strategies to stop him, and frequently had as many as three men guarding him, but nothing could keep Don Hutson in check. His instinct for following and catching forward passes, his keen timing, and his knack of being in the right spot at the right moment, were too much for the most alert of rival defensemen. His receiving of forward passes was so uncanny and magnificent that he drove rival players and coaches to distraction.

One of his favorite strategic moves, when he was double- and triple-teamed, was so fantastic that old-timers still talk about it. For as touchdown-crazed Hutson ran at top speed for the goal line with rival defenders all around him, he would hook his arm around the goal post in such a fashion that his momentum would twirl him away from the defenders, and Don would stretch out his other free arm to snare the pass. Once, during a single quarter of play, he set an all-time record by scoring 29 points.

As the greatest of ends, the stringbean-slim Don Hutson played his position both ways — defensive as well as an offensive end. He was a dependable tackler, and even more, he was a skilled place-kicker. Once, he even led the league in field goals.

Don Hutson's versatility and adaptability as football's greatest end bordered on the unbelievable, but in his eleven glorious years in pro football, he made all believe that he was one of a kind.

In 1945, at the age of thirty-two, he suddenly decided that he had had enough of gridiron glory, and he quit playing. But he remains "the end" for the ages — football's greatest end.

"THE FOUR HORSEMEN"
They Galloped Into Immortality

One of the remarkable things about the Four Horsemen of Notre Dame, football's greatest and most widely heralded backfield in history, was that none of the four was a big man. Halfbacks James Crowley and Donald Miller weighed 162 pounds each. Fullback Elmer Layden weighed 160 pounds. Quarterback Harry Stuhldreher weighed barely 154. Yet, over a three-year period (1922, 1923, 1924), they took on the best college teams in the country and tore rival lines into shreds, winning twenty-seven games, losing two, and tying one. With the Four Horsemen riding wildly on the gridirons of the land, Notre Dame was acclaimed national champion over that period. The Four Horsemen did more than win national championships — they pioneered modern football. With their daring, matchless exploits, they brought a new excitement to the game. Other colleges throughout the land strove to reach the Notre Dame level of winning football.

Harry Stuhldreher, Jim Crowley, Don Miller, and Elmer Layden first came together as sophomores on the 1922 Irish football squad. There had been no special heralding of their arrival, and, in fact, coach Knute Rockne wasn't overly impressed with any of the four when he saw them for the first time. Stuhldreher, the quarterback who was a genius at calling plays in addition to being a fearless blocker, did not make first string until the season was under way. Although Layden and Crowley were both speedsters who could run, kick, and pass, they shared a backfield spot for the first part of that year. And it was not until midseason when Miller, a compact and slippery ball carrier, joined the others in the backfield.

When those four unknown sophomores got into a game as a unit for the first time, they became inseparable as a first-string backfield for Notre Dame. To Knute Rockne's surprise, the four meshed in mind and body to become the greatest, the most destructive, and the most colorful backfield in football history.

They showed their incomparable artistry in a game against a mighty Army team from West Point in New York in 1924. Notre Dame won that game because its pony backfield ran with a machinelike precision and rhythm never seen before on a football field. With awesome speed and grace each part fitted smoothly into an effort and execution that left an indelible imprint on all who witnessed that titanic gridiron contest. It prompted the famous poet-scribe Grantland Rice, king of American sportswriters, to begin his newspaper story the next day like this:

POLO GROUNDS, N.Y., OCTOBER 18, 1924
——Outlined against a blue-gray October sky, the Four Horsemen rode again. In dramatic lore they

The "Four Horsemen" of Notre Dame: (Left to right) Don Miller, Harry Stuhldreher, Jim Crowley, Elmer Layden.

are known as Famine, Pestilence, Destruction and Death. These are only aliases. Their real names are Stuhldreher, Miller, Crowley and Layden. They formed the crest of the South Bend cyclone before which another fighting Army football team was swept over the precipice of the Polo Grounds yesterday afternoon as 55,000 spectators peered down on the bewildering panorama spread on the green plain below.

The Notre Dame student publicity man at the time was a man named George Strickler, and he was clever enough to see the gold in the nickname. He posed the four backs on horseback and the photograph became one of the most widely reproduced sports pictures of all time. And they lived up to their press notices.

The fabled quartet had arrived at Notre Dame by different routes. Don Miller, from Cleveland, Ohio, was the fourth in a line of Miller brothers who played football at South Bend. Stuhldreher also had a brother at Notre Dame, a nonathletic upperclassman. Crowley had been coached at East Green Bay, Wisconsin, by Earl ("Curly") Lambeau (later coach of the Packers, the Green Bay pro team). Layden was coached in high school in Davenport, Iowa, by Walter Halas, who became track and baseball coach at Notre Dame and who wanted Layden for those sports. But after Rockne got him, he was strictly a football man.

Perhaps the Four Horsemen reached their galloping best in their senior year against Nebraska, Notre Dame's most persistent challenger in those days. The "perfect backfield" was just too much for the Cornhuskers, who were beaten 34-6. Crowley sprinted 80 yards for one score and Layden sliced through the line at will. Stuhldreher passed the Nebraska secondary dizzy. Miller was a quiet tiger as he piled up yardage. It was a typical Horsemen performance, supported, of course, by the tremendous line, nicknamed by this time the Seven Mules. Notre Dame swept through nine opponents in similar fashion that year, and for the Four Horsemen's last game together, the team accepted an invitation to the 1925 Rose Bowl to play in Pasadena on New Year's Day against the Pacific Coast champion, a mighty Stanford University football team, led by the immortal fullback, Ernie Nevers. It was the Four Horsemen's one and only trip to the famed Rose Bowl classic.

The Four Horsemen were too clever, too swift, and too elusive for Stanford. The Four Horsemen pulverized that rugged Stanford team to win the national championship with ease by a score of 27-10. That victory gave Notre Dame a football eminence the university has maintained ever since.

When the renowned and fabulous Four Horsemen left Notre Dame to ride off into immortality, coach Knute Rockne waxed more poetic than usual.

"How it came to pass," he marveled, "that four young men so eminently qualified by temperament, physique and instinctive pacing, complemented one another perfectly and produced the best coordinated and most picturesque backfield in the history of football. How that came about is one of the inscrutable achievements of coincidence of which I know nothing save that it's a rather satisfying mouthful of words."

Rockne said a mouthful, all right — and all of it was true. For the legendary Four Horsemen left an imprint on football that has never been equaled. Their name will endure.

BYRON ("WHIZZER") WHITE
The Man in the Black Robe

Before Byron Raymond ("Whizzer") White came along, the average big-time college football player was envisioned as a behemoth of a man who had trouble solving long-division problems. But in 1937, White burst on the collegiate football scene like a meteor. He was not only acclaimed by everybody as All-America halfback, but he also achieved Phi Beta Kappa status as a student and was brilliant enough to win a Rhodes Scholarship to study at Oxford University in England.

Such braininess for a gridder was practically unheard-of even in the Ivy League colleges, Yale, Harvard, and Princeton. But White came from the tiny University of Colorado, and this added to the Whizzer's fame as a "glamour boy" of football. Although he weighed only 187 pounds and stood barely over six feet tall, he was exactly what his name implied: a whiz at running with a football.

White was a fast and elusive runner, a superb passer and kicker and, in those days of sixty-minute players, a destructive tackler. He led all major college players in scoring, rushing and total offense in his senior year — making 16 touchdowns, kicking 25 conversions, completing 22 passes for 314 yards, running back kicks for 731 yards, and kicking the longest punt of the year, 84 yards in the air. In carrying the ball 181 times,

he gained 1,121 yards and scored a season's record of 103 points.

The most famous Eastern sportswriter of the day took White's press clippings with a touch of cynicism and went out himself to take a look. He saw White and his Colorado teammates squash powerful Utah, 17-7, with White scoring all 17 points; that writer became a believer in the wizardry of the Whizzer.

"Utah was leading, 7-3, when the fourth period opened," he wrote, "and the partisan crowd of more than 20,000 had high hopes for Utah's first victory over Colorado in three years. But on the first play of this period White took a high punt on his own 12-yard line and never stopped until the last stripe was crossed. As he caught the ball, six Utah men surrounded him and drove him back to his own 5-yard line, and apparently pinned him in a corner. But they couldn't put their hands on him. Twisting, squirming, ducking and dodging, he eluded them and set out down the sidelines. Once in the clear, he put on full speed and simply outran his pursuers."

Breathless newspaper accounts of this sort attracted the attention of the professional scouts. After his college days were over, All-America White decided to take a fling at the rugged game of professional football.

He was signed by the Pittsburgh Steelers of the National Football League for the 1938 season at the then unprecedented salary (for a rookie) of $15,000. If there were any skeptics left, they were soon silenced by White's prowess on the fields of the NFL. Though only a rookie, Whizzer was the leading ground-gainer in the league.

Even fans in his home town of Fort Collins, Colorado, where he was born in 1917, were surprised at his exploits. And they were even more astonished when, after that brilliant rookie year, he announced he was quitting the game to take advantage of his Rhodes Scholarship at Oxford. His gridiron bosses pleaded with him to reconsider and to continue to play ball, but White had his eye on higher goals.

When he returned to the United States in 1940, White again played professional football, this time with the Detroit Lions. He hadn't lost his swivel touch. Again he led the National Football League in ground-gaining (514 yards in 146 carries), and he was named All-Pro halfback for 1940. He played again for the Lions the next year, but he also attended Yale Law School.

Both his education and his football exploits were interrupted by service in the United States Navy as a PT boat commander in the South Pacific during World War II. When he returned in 1946, White was urged to return to the grid wars for his fame and fortune. But he rejected all offers, won his law degree at Yale, and eventually returned to Denver, in his home state, to practice law.

Obscurity was not the fate of that football great, however. Years later, the game's one-time glamour boy was still an unusual pacemaker for gridiron glory. For when Hall-of-Famer Whizzer White was

only forty-four years old, he gained the highest eminence ever achieved by a famous football player. The President of the United States named him a justice of the highest court in the land. He became the youngest justice to sit on the bench of the United States Supreme Court.

For the football world it represented the greatest national honor ever bestowed upon one of its gridiron heroes.

JOHN VICTOR McNALLY
Nobody Was Like Johnny Blood

High on the charter list of members of the Professional Football Hall of Fame at Canton, Ohio, is the name of John Victor McNally. He is better known as Johnny Blood, and he was one of the most spectacular and unpredictable halfbacks of them all. He played for such teams as the Milwaukee Badgers, the Duluth Eskimos, and the Pottsville Maroons in the early days of pro football, and in eight years with the Green Bay Packers he scored 224 points and helped them win four National Football League championships. Later, he was player-coach for the Pittsburgh Steelers, and when he left the game in 1939, he had bequeathed it a catalog of exploits that have never been forgotten. For sixteen seasons he had played a lot of extraordinary football.

He was one of the greatest characters of pro football.

McNally could do anything with a football, but he was at his best in pass receiving. He thought there wasn't a ball in the air he couldn't catch. As a runner, he had extraordinary speed, swivel hips, and a change of pace that would fake defensive backs out of their shoes. He was a great improviser, and when the designated hole in the line didn't materialize, he often made up a substitute play on the spot, usually for good yardage. And off the field he was such an irrepressible spirit that old-timers still tell tales of his antics.

He was a magnificent screwball.

Once, in an effort to get spending money from his coach, McNally hung outside the coach's hotel room window, eight stories high, almost giving the coach heart failure. On another occasion he balanced himself on the railing of a train's observation car to prove some point or other. At times, he also entertained and stirred large street-corner crowds with rousing poems and literary recitations.

He was born in New Richmond, Wisconsin, around the turn of the century. A precocious boy, he was graduated from high school at the tender age of fourteen, but he had been too small to play any kind of sport. A few years later, though, he filled out, and when he attended a small Benedictine college, St. John's, in Collegeville, Minnesota, he was a four-letter man in football, baseball, track and basketball. Later, he became something of a tramp college athlete, as was common in those days, jumping from school to school and playing under different names.

That was how he picked up the nickname "Johnny Blood." He and a St. John's classmate both had a year of eligibility left when they heard that a professional team was being organized in Minneapolis. They decided to try out for the squad, but in deference to St. John's they applied under false names. As they rode out to the ball park, they passed a movie theater advertising a Rudolph Valentino film, *Blood and Sand*. "That's it," Johnny said to his friend. "There are our names. I'll be Blood and you be Sand." He made the team and never went back to St. John's; he did attend Notre Dame for a while, but did not play there. He later played for a pro team in Ironwood, Michigan, and another in Milwaukee. Then he became quarterback for Ernie Nevers' Duluth Eskimos, and he is still remembered as one of the finest quarterbacks of that early era.

In 1928 he joined the Green Bay Packers and became the outstanding pass receiver in the league, operating from a wingback position.

Blood left the Packers to become coach-player for the Pittsburgh Steelers in 1937. One of his players was Byron ("Whizzer") White, the Colorado All-America who later became a U. S. Supreme Court justice. They were close friends, as well as teammates.

In his time, Johnny Blood was a household word. To countless teen-agers he was a football hero out of fiction. None of them ever forgot his name when they grew into manhood.

Many years after Johnny Blood had quit playing football, he came to the nation's capital to attend a White House reception. When John McNally was presented to John F. Kennedy, then President of the United States, the youthful Chief Executive greeted him with boyish enthusiasm and admiration.

"I remember you, Johnny Blood," said President Kennedy. "Your name was a household word in our home."

It was shortly before World War II when that legendary halfback finally quit playing football and roamed on to other fields and other pursuits. He became an Air Force staff sergeant for war duty in India and China. For a while he read law as a clerk in a law firm, tended bar in a San Francisco saloon, was a croupier in a gambling house, a hotel desk clerk, a seaman, a miner, a farmhand, a feed salesman, a pick-and-shovel laborer, a floor waxer, a newspaper stereotyper, and a sportswriter. He also ran for sheriff of St. Croix County in Wisconsin, taught history and economics at St. John's University in Minnesota, and at the age of fifty enrolled at the University of Minnesota to study for a master's degree.

The incredible Johnny Blood must have left his mark on all those occupations, but not as indelible as the one he left on the game of professional football. The kind of football he had played earned for him the imperishable fame of being included in the first exclusive band of immortal gridiron heroes chosen for enshrinement in pro football's Hall of Fame at Canton, Ohio, where professional football first began.

GLENN SCOBEY ("POP") WARNER
The Great White Football Father

The only coach in football history who was ever known as the "Great White Football Father" was Pop Warner, the only man to coach a college football team composed entirely of Indian players. And with his amazing gridiron Indians, coach Warner created the Carlisle legend — the most incredible and fascinating legend of gridiron glory in American college football.

Never was there another college in the United States like Carlisle, and never was there another football coach quite like Pop Warner who, at the little Indian school in Carlisle, Pennsylvania, created football teams for intercollegiate gridiron warfare that will never fade from memory.

It was 1899 when Pop Warner was hired as head football coach at Carlisle for the munificent salary of thirty-five dollars a week. He was a one-man coaching staff. Many of the stalwart young American Indians from all tribes who began playing for coach Pop Warner had never even seen a football until they came to Carlisle. Nevertheless, it didn't take long for coach Warner to guide tiny Carlisle College from football obscurity to fame. Under his artful and wily coaching, the football-minded Redskins absorbed their grid lessons so quickly and well that the Carlisle football team became the scourge of the collegiate football world. Playing against the outstanding college teams, the Carlisle Indians toppled the giants of the game with devastating regularity. Capitalizing upon the Indians' recklessness, durability, clever trickery, and pride, coach Warner instilled a team spirit among his players so inspiring that it made Carlisle football teams almost invincible. They produced some of the most unbelievable upsets in college football history. In some seasons, Pop's Indians rolled up almost 500 points against grid opponents.

Since coach Warner rarely had a football squad numbering more than sixteen men, every player had to be good and versatile — able to play any position, and play sixty minutes of every football game. Tough and exacting, he worked his Indian players hard, but they loved every minute of it. To all his players he was the "Great White Football Father."

Pop Warner never punished erring players, and never had to take disciplinary action against anyone. The players themselves administered swift and Spartan justice to any Carlisle football warrior who broke training rules. The culprit was taken into the gymnasium and denuded of his trousers. Then every man on the team filed in front of him, and each gave him two solid blows, with doubled fists, on his bare thighs. The transgressor sometimes was unable to walk for hours after that ordeal.

The procession of great football players that came out of tiny Carlisle College under the coaching genius of Pop Warner dwarfed the output of any other college in America. Season after season, at least one Carlisle player was acclaimed All-American. Of course, the most fabulous All-American wonder Pop Warner developed at Carlisle was the legendary Jim Thorpe, who to this day is accepted by all the historians of the game as the greatest football player of all time.

At Carlisle, coach Warner was not only a football pioneer, but also an incomparable gridiron strategist when it came to invention and innovation. He conceived the double wing formation, the crouch start, the numbering of plays, the hidden ball trick, and the spiral punt, among other grid novelties.

Unique and legendary were the locker-room pep talks he gave his Indian players before important games. The most unforgettable one ever delivered by a college football coach happened before the final game of the 1912 season, when the Carlisle Indians came to West Point to play against a mighty undefeated Army team acclaimed by all as the national college champions. The powerful Cadets were an overwhelming favorite to win by several touchdowns. But wily coach Pop Warner stirred up his players with the strangest locker-room pep talk ever heard.

"From the shores of Little Big Horn to the banks of Wounded Knee Creek, the spirits of your people call to you," Pop Warner told his players. "The men who died in Chief Joseph's retreat over the mountains, the Cherokees who marched on bleeding feet through the snow out of their ancestral lands, tell you that you must win. These men you will play

against are soldiers. They are the Long Knives. You are Indians. Today we will know whether or not you are warriors!''

Carlisle crushed Army under a lopsided score.

With a flair for the spectacular, coach Warner was football's first showman. He was the first college coach to have his players wear numbers on their jerseys. His Carlisle football team was the first college team to have a student band to play at games, and have a rooting section of glamour girls to cheer for the players. They were the Indian maiden students of Carlisle. Pop Warner gave college football its first packed stadium.

However, the incredible saga Pop Warner created during his illustrious years at Carlisle, coaching Indians to imperishable college football glories, came to an end in 1918, when Carlisle College ceased to exist. At the time, the country was involved in the first World War, and the United States War Department converted the famed Indian school into a military hospital.

Pop Warner went on to other colleges to coach football teams to victory. He coached at Pittsburgh University where he guided the Panthers to several undefeated seasons. Then he went out west to coach at Stanford University, where his football teams had many glorious winning seasons and Rose Bowl fame.

In all, Pop Warner was a football coach at six different colleges, in a fabulous career that stretched over forty-four years. As a college coach, he compiled an astonishing winning record of 313 victories. When he died on September 7, 1954, at the age of 83, he left behind one of the greatest coaching reputations ever achieved by any immortal college football coach now enshrined in the National College Football Hall of Fame.

As long as the amazing legend of the Carlisle Indians glows in college football history, coach Pop Warner, the ''Great White Football Father'' of Carlisle, will be remembered as the gridiron genius who created it.

JOSEPH NAPOLEON GUYON
Second Best to the Very Best

In football's early years, around the turn of the century, there were many fine and outstanding Indian players. All came out of that unique little school for higher learning at Carlisle, Pennsylvania, which forever will live in gridiron legends as Carlisle College. Of course, the most renowned Carlisle Indian player of all was the immortal Jim Thorpe, acclaimed by all historians to this day as the greatest football player of all time.

A one-time Carlisle teammate of the legendary Jim Thorpe who was regarded as the second greatest Indian football player in history was Joe Guyon.

A full-blooded Indian of the Chippewa tribe, he was born in 1892 on a reservation in Minnesota. His Indian name was *O-Gee-Chidaha*, which meant "brave man," and Indian Joe Guyon lived up to that name when he appeared on the football scene to make gridiron history as a college and professional player.

At Carlisle College, Indian Joe was magnificent in his own right as a college football wonder. No player was swifter in gridiron warfare, no blocker was more devastating, no tackler was more violent, no passer was more accurate than the 179-pound Carlisle halfback. Indian Joe also was an astonishing punter. He succeeded Jim Thorpe as an All-America football hero from Carlisle College.

But later, Indian Joe grew restless basking in the glory of Carlisle football fame,

and he transferred to play college football at Georgia Tech. There, his matchless all-around playing not only sparked the 1917 Georgia Tech team to nine victories and an undefeated season, but also to the glory of a national college football championship. (Indian Joe Guyon was enshrined in the National College Football Hall of Fame as a gridiron immortal in 1966.)

Even greater gridiron fame awaited Indian Joe after his glorious college playing days were over. His one-time Carlisle teammate and friend, Jim Thorpe, invited

him to become a pro football player and join the famed Canton Bulldogs. That was in 1918, three years before the National Football League was founded.

Again, Indian Joe was phenomenal as an all-around football player. In the three years he starred for the Canton Bulldogs, they never lost a single game.

But even as a pro player, Indian Joe was restless, and he changed teams on impulse, always playing for the highest bidder. Though his professional football career was relatively short, he played for seven different clubs. He starred for the Buffalo Bisons, the Kansas City Cowboys, the Cleveland Indians, the Oorang Indians, and the Rock Island Independents — great and bone-crushing pro teams in their time. But wherever Indian Joe played, he was a brilliant star, indestructible on both offense and defense.

In 1927, he finished his pro career with the New York Giants. His magnificent playing that season not only sparked them to eleven victories, but also to their first pro football championship.

Indian Joe was perhaps the trickiest football player ever. The most unforgettable demonstration of his foxiness on the gridiron warpath occurred when he was starring for the New York Giants. One afternoon, the Giants met the powerful Chicago Bears in a most decisive game. It was one of the most violent pro games ever played. Playing for the Bears in that game was George Halas, a feared end. His bone-crunching playing had put a host of opponents out of commission.

In the third quarter, Indian Joe drifted back to pass, but tough George Halas quickly leaped to strike down the Indian with his standard violence. Halas came tearing in on Indian Joe's blind side, in-

tent to dump him with enthusiasm. Guyon's back was to Halas as Halas made his move to put the famous Indian out of commission. But just as Halas reached his target, Indian Joe whirled around and swung a knee that caught Halas in the chest. At the same time, Indian Joe fell backward, screaming that George Halas had clipped him.

While Halas was being carried from the field — unconscious and with four broken ribs — curiously, the referee agreed with Indian Joe and penalized the Bears 15 yards for clipping! That penalty helped the Giants score the winning touchdown.

Later, Indian Joe consoled injured Chicago end Halas by gently telling him: "George, you should know better than to try to sneak up on an Indian." It was a lesson George Halas, who later became the owner and foremost coach of the Chicago Bears, never forgot.

Indian Joe Guyon quit playing pro football in 1927. He left behind him such impressive credentials for his fame that he gained enshrinement in the National Professional Football Hall of Fame as one of the immortals of the pro game.

Joe Guyon was only the second Indian football player in history to achieve immortality twice — as an honored member of a National Football Hall of Fame, both as a college and pro gridiron wonder.

He never stopped idolizing his onetime Carlisle teammate and close friend, the legendary Jim Thorpe, as the greatest football player of all time. And whenever people praised Joe Guyon, and told him that he was the second best Indian player in history to have played college and pro football, Indian Joe was at his proudest moment.

After Thorpe's death in 1953, it was

Indian Joe who did most to help establish the Thorpe Memorial in Pennsylvania, near where once stood famed Carlisle College, home of the greatest Indian football players ever. Thorpe's shrine has become world-famous to keep green the memory of the greatest athlete America ever had.

Joseph Napoleon Guyon, best known as Indian Joe, died in 1971. He left this world with a unique distinction — the last survivor of those amazing American Indians who created the unforgettable Carlisle College legend.

MARION MOTLEY
The First Black Pro Immortal

When Marion Motley was playing football at Canton's McKinley High School, he was an outstanding schoolboy athlete in Ohio. But he went on to greater fame as a football hero at the University of Nevada, where he set grid records galore and won All-America honors as one of the most explosive fullbacks ever seen in intercollegiate football.

He hooked up with the Cleveland Browns for his big-league pro career, and as a pile-driving and indestructible fullback he had many years of pro greatness. Power and speed were his stock in trade. His magnificent playing sparked the Browns to football championships again and again. Once in a game, he averaged 17.09 yards per carry, for a National Football League record. In his eight seasons in the pro game, he carried the ball 826 times for 4,712 yards, an average of 5.7 yards per carry. Motley was incomparable as a running or blocking back. Injuries finally stopped his spectacular and awesome rushes to

glory, and in 1955 he quit pro football as a player.

He gained a unique distinction in professional football for his everlasting fame. He is the first black to have won enshrinement in the Pro Football Hall of Fame at Canton, Ohio, as an immortal of the game.

MEL HEIN
The Indestructible Center

In old-timers' bull sessions, when the subject of all-time great linemen comes up, the name Mel Hein almost invariably leads the list. The big man — he stood six feet, four inches, and weighed 230 pounds — was center for the New York Giants for fifteen bruising years and ranks with the immortals of the game.

Among the other awesome credentials Hein brought to the Hall of Fame was the fact that he revolutionized the way of playing center. He was fast and agile, a tower of strength, but he was not content, the way most centers were in those days, just to snap the ball back. Hein went forward, knocking down linebackers and other defenders. He was the first center to start pulling out of the line to run interference for his runners. He was the first to drop back and protect the passer from the rushes of the opposing linemen. On defense, he was a marvel, too. He was the first center to start roaming behind the line of scrimmage. Until his time, centers stayed up close watching for line bucks in the middle. But Mel was too fast for this kind of dull defensive play. He fell back to cover on short passes; he ranged out on the ends, pulling down runners. And when runners came off tackle, they were met with some of the most savage tackles the game ever saw.

Yet, as ferociously as he played, he was never a dirty player. He never slug-

ged, kneed, gouged, or piled on a downed player, but when Hein tackled them, they stayed tackled. He was nicknamed "Old Indestructible," for in his fifteen years as a pro and eight years in high school and college he never missed a game. Even in his last year in pro ranks, at the age of thirty-six, he was still turning in sixty-minute performances.

Melvin John Hein was born in California, but his family moved to the state of Washington when he was a small boy. For a while they lived in the mountains, until settling down in Glacier, a town too small to be on a map.

Although young Hein had never seen a football, basketball, or regulation baseball game, he caught on quickly. At Fairhaven High, he played a different position each year, in order: guard, center, halfback, tackle. He also participated in basketball, baseball, and track. At Washington State College, at Pullman, he played center on the freshman team in 1927, and for the varsity the following three years. In his senior year (1930) he was described as an inspirational captain as he led his team to the Pacific Coast Conference championship and a trip to the Rose Bowl. Hein made All-America in his senior year and the college retired his famed "Number 7"; his jersey is enshrined in the trophy room at Pullman.

He continued to wear Number 7 when he joined the pros and the Giants the following year. Almost immediately he was a standout. His size, coupled with his speed and agility, and his quick mind, made him a linebacker and center of superlative quality. In fifteen years in the big leagues, Hein was named All-Pro center eight times. Each year he seemed to become more adept. One year (1938) he was named the National League's Most Valuable Player, the only lineman (exclusive of ends) ever to attain that honor.

As he grew wiser to the ways of the league, Hein became a spectacular defender.

Steve Owen, who coached the Giants throughout Hein's glamorous career, once said that Mel required very little coaching.

The Giants perfected a play in which Hein was on the end of the line, and hence eligible in those days to receive a forward pass. (The rule has been changed since.) Hein would snap the ball to quarterback Harry Newman, who passed it right back to him. Then, while Newman feinted passes to the backs, Hein would jog down the field — 10, 20, sometimes 30 yards — before it was discovered that he had the ball.

In 1940, when Hein marked his tenth year as a Giant, the management held a "Mel Hein Day" at the Polo Grounds. Hein retired two years later and became a coach at Union College in Schenectady, New York. But the Giants wanted him back during the war years because of a shortage of skilled players, and Old Number 7 came out of retirement. He arrived in Boston for the opening game of the season. He'd had no training, no time to get in shape. But Mel was never out of shape. He played sixty minutes of football that first game and sixty minutes every game thereafter. He finally retired for good after the 1945 season.

The Giants, as had Washington State College before them, retired Number 7. No Giant player will ever again sport that jersey number, for it is likely that no Giant player, nor any other player on any other football team, will ever again perform as valiantly at the center post as did the indestructible pacemaker Mel Hein, the greatest center football ever had.

JOSEPH WILLIE NAMATH
Super Joe

No football player in history ever lived a finer day of gridiron glory than Joe Namath on the afternoon of January 12, 1969. In Miami's famed Orange Bowl, before an audience of more than seventy million people watching him at the ballpark and on television screens, he performed a gridiron miracle, proving that he was as outstanding a quarterback as ever played the game.

Almost single-handedly, with matchless field generalship and astonishing forward passes, he engineered the most unbelievable upset victory in pro football history, leading the underdog New York Jets of the new American Football League to a Super Bowl triumph over the overwhelmingly favored Baltimore Colts of the proud old National Football League. It was the first time any team from the supposedly inferior American Football League had tasted the glory of a Super Bowl victory and won the pro football championship of the world.

As the architect of that miracle triumph, quarterback Namath not only put a whole football league on the map, but also caused a revolution in the structure of the game of big-time professional football. The stunning upset victory eventually forced the NFL to merge with the AFL — both to play major pro football as equals.

On that unforgettable football day, quarterback Joe Namath, with his magnificent heroics in the annual Super Bowl contest, established himself in popular imagination as the most glamorous and most fabulous player in pro football history. He became, indeed, an American folk hero.

That glory pedestal was a long way from Joe Namath's humble beginnings in the drab steel town of Beaver Falls, Pennsylvania, where he was born on May 31, 1943, the son of an immigrant steel worker.

Small, skinny, but spunky, he was only five years old when he first began throwing a football around with his three older brothers. Growing up in soot-soiled Beaver Falls, little Joe was a restless and wild youngster who enjoyed getting into mischief. He ran the streets with a gang of dead-end kids ever on the hunt for trouble. Sometimes, to earn a few dollars, he shined shoes, caddied at the local golf club, and did odd jobs. But he also found time to play football. At Beaver Falls Area High School he became such a skilled and outstanding quarterback, and he set so many noteworthy schoolboy grid records, that no less than one-hundred colleges throughout the United States offered him athletic scholarships upon his graduation.

Joe Namath wound up at the University of Alabama, playing football under the

tutelage of Paul ("Bear") Bryant, one of the most illustrious college coaches. Though Namath was a "showboat" and playboy (once he actually was kicked off the team for ignoring training rules), his gridiron feats for the Crimson Tide brought him national prominence as one of the finest quarterbacks in intercollegiate football competition.

In 1965, when his glorious college

football years were done, quarterback Namath achieved eminence as a unique football hero. He invaded the violent world of pro football in such a spectacular manner that it astonished an entire nation. The New York Jets of the American Football League snared him for the largest bonus and salary ever offered a rookie pro football player — $427,000.

In no time at all, Joe Namath became the most glamorous, most exciting, most controversial, and most talked-about player. With his spectacular doings on and off the field, he stood out above all other competition.

Reveling in the limelight of his ever-growing fame, "Super Joe," as he came to be known, lived in luxurious bachelor splendor, sported a full wardrobe of the latest clothes, wore a $5,000 mink fur coat to keep him warm, drove the swankiest and most expensive cars, dated the most beautiful girls, and held court in New York's most famous night clubs. His swinging life style earned him the nickname of "Broadway Joe." In time, he became a motion picture star and a celebrity performer on television shows. He also became involved in numerous business matters. All of that transformed the once-poor boy from Beaver Falls into a millionaire.

Incredible as Joe Namath was off a football field, he was equally incredible on it. No quarterback was ever craftier nor more football-wise. He was as marvelous a thrower of forward passes as ever played the game. His skills were phenomenal, and often he threw unbelievable bulls'-eye passes which produced startling results and astonishing victories for his team.

Blessed with exceptionally sharp eyes, and an amazingly quick release of his forward passes, he pitched accurately to his receivers even when enemy tacklers were only inches away. One season he threw for 26 touchdown passes, and in 1967 he became the first quarterback in history to gain 4,000 yards with forward passes (actually, 4,007) in one football year. As the seasons went by, numerous honors were bestowed upon Broadway Joe to enrich his claim and fame as the premier quarterback in pro football.

But his matchless skills did not spare him physical punishment. Because he often bragged about what he was going to do before important games — and then went out and did it — driving enemy defenders seemed to take special delight in tackling Namath and viciously pounding him into the turf, even when he had let go of the ball. As a result, Super Joe began to suffer with the pains and miseries of injured knees, and there were times when he had to undergo surgery, losing valuable playing-time over the football seasons.

Nevertheless, in his first eight seasons in the pro ranks, he compiled a most impressive record of glory as a fabulous quarterback marvel. He had thrown forward passes for more than 21,000 yards, and for 126 touchdowns.

Despite ailing, painful knees, Joe Namath's love for football-play never slackened. At the age of thirty, he was still starring for the New York Jets, and still trying to prove that he was the best of all big-league pro quarterbacks. He was still the highest-paid player in pro football history, for he commanded a season's salary of more than a quarter of a million dollars. Moreover, he was still football's most glamorous, most exciting, most controversial, and most famous player. Quarterback Joe Willie Namath had become a legend in his own time.

CHUCK BEDNARIK
The Two-Way Pro

The amazing story of Chuck Bednarik reached its high point in 1960 when, at the age of thirty-six (an advanced age for a professional football player), he led the Philadelphia Eagles to the world's championship. He battled as no modern football player has ever battled; he played a ferocious game both as offensive center and as middle linebacker. He was a two-way man in an age of specialization.

That season was climaxed in the championship game at Philadelphia's Franklin Field, with the Eagles leading the Green Bay Packers 17-13 and only one play remaining. The Packers were in a huddle, shaping strategy for their final chance. Quarterback Bart Starr tossed a flat pass to the Packers' fullback, Jim Taylor, and Taylor started churning toward the Eagle goal as Eagle defenders bounced off his body. At the 10-yard line, Bednarik took his best shot. Two bodies collided with the title hanging in the balance. Then Taylor went down, Bednarik atop him. A second passed — and the gun went off. It was Chuck's finest moment in a fourteen-year career that was crowded with fine moments.

Charles Bednarik was born in Bethlehem, Pennsylvania, son of a steelworker. In high school he was a three-sport man: football, basketball, and baseball. On the gridiron he was a burly fullback until an emergency arose, and overnight his coach assigned him to center. He was outstanding. After graduation, he went into the Air Force and he came out a well-decorated combat waist-gunner, twenty years old and ready for college. Upon the advice of his high-school coach, he entered the University of Pennsylvania on the GI Bill of Rights.

Bednarik played four hard-tackling years as Penn's regular center, made All-America twice, and was singled out as the best college football player in the country in 1948 when he won the Maxwell Award. The Eagles drafted him that year and offered him a contract. He signed with the Eagles, probably because of his successes at Penn. It wasn't long before he was recognized as one of the top bruising linebackers in the pros. In his rookie year, the Eagles won their third straight title, but they were not to win again for another decade.

It wasn't Chuck's fault they didn't. Between 1950 and 1960 he was All-Pro linebacker eight times. He played for half a dozen Eagle head coaches over that period: Greasy Neale, Walt Kiesling, Bo McMillin, Wayne Millner, Jim Trimble, and Buck Shaw. They were unanimous in their praise for his crunching defensive play. But as the years rolled on, Bednarik became offensive center and he was a standout at that post, too. He was still a center when the championship year started, but at training camp, coach Buck Shaw suggested that he also practice with the defense, "just in case something happens."

It happened in the Eagles' fifth game of the season, a tough match against the Browns in Cleveland. Linebacker Bob Pellegrini went down in a heap and was knocked out of the game. "Hey, Chuck," Shaw yelled, "get in there! Pelly's hurt." So Bednarik grabbed his helmet and ran onto the field. Except for kickoff and punt returns, he was never out of a game from then on. "It's a funny feeling," Chuck said. "The ball would change hands. Twenty-one guys would go running off the field, and there I would be, alone, waiting. It's hard to describe, staying out there with only the officials."

From then on, Chuck was a sixty-minute man. His tireless efforts lifted the Eagles from being a so-so club to being the champions.

Perhaps the key game in that pennant-winning season was the one against the New York Giants at Yankee Stadium. It was generally decided by the experts that the game would settle the Eastern Division title. It was a whale of an exciting game, and in the fourth period the Eagles were ahead, 17-10, but the Giants were moving down the field with plenty of time to catch up. Frank Gifford, the Giants' star halfback, started through an opening in the Eagle line, when from his linebacker position, Bednarik tackled him so viciously that Gifford fumbled and the Eagles recovered. There were a good many complaints about the play, some people claiming that it was a blind-side tackle. But Gifford himself never said so. Gifford said: "I've never resented the way you hit me. It was a good clean tackle. You've always been tough, but you're clean, buddy." Bednarik, who despite his rough play had never been called a dirty player in his entire career, was delighted to get that accolade from an opposing star.

Bednarik signed a contract for the 1961 season and told newsmen that it would be his last. Again he played both ways, but he was thirty-seven years old and age was telling. Nevertheless, he changed his mind about retiring and played another full season in 1962, and then he hung up the big Number 60 that had served football in Philadelphia so valiantly for eighteen years.

He was a pacemaker, all right, and he set a pace that may never be equaled in the game of professional football.

CAL HUBBARD
The Perfect Tackle

Cal Hubbard, who is considered the perfect tackle by most football historians, was a giant of a man. As a professional gridder, he stood 6 feet, 5 inches, weighed 265 pounds, and played a bone-crushing game. But it was not his size alone that impressed the experts. He was extremely fast (he could run 100 yards in eleven seconds), mobile, and aggressive, and he dominated any game he ever played in college or pro ball. Besides this, he was one of the first "policemen" in pro ranks, his duties being to rough up an enemy player who was getting away with "dirty" tactics. Hubbard, who was level-headed and even-tempered, was such a successful policeman that when he took summary action against a fouling opponent, players, fans, and officials all recognized that the fouler had done something to merit his punishment.

Robert Calvin Hubbard was born on October 31, 1900, on a farm in Keytesville, Missouri, and by the time he reached high school he had already developed into a 200-pounder. Although he had a great love for baseball, Cal found that his weight could be used to greater advantage on the gridiron. His football idol was Alvin ("Bo") McMillin, who had been captain of the Praying Colonels, the famed little Centre College team from Kentucky which had upset mighty Harvard in the upset of the century. McMillin had gone into coaching ranks and was head man at Centenary College, a tiny school in Louisiana. Hubbard made his way there and played end and tackle on a McMillin team that won ten games. Although he was only a freshman and from an unheard-of college, Hubbard was named on many All-America teams. He won more honors as a sophomore. Then Bo McMillin became head coach at Geneva College in Beaver Falls, Pennsylvania, and along went Hubbard to play for his idol. He again made All-America and participated in some dazzling upsets Geneva pulled off against unsuspecting larger colleges.

After he was graduated, Cal signed as a pro with the New York Giants for the 1927 season. He received only $150 a game, indicative of the low wage scale prevailing at the time. Hubbard almost immediately became one of the great tackles in the league. For two years he played in thirty-four games with the Giants, missing only two minutes of play once because of a cracked bone. But Cal, being a farm boy, wasn't happy with the big city of New York and he requested the owners to trade him to Green Bay, a little community in Wisconsin farming territory more to his liking.

At Green Bay, Hubbard reached the peak of his game. He was used as linebacker on defense at first, but later shifted to tackle. He won All-League honors in both posts, for it was generally conceded that there wasn't a better lineman in the game. With his commanding performances on both offense and defense, the Packers won the championship title three years in a row. Old-timers still recall how he racked up opposing ball carriers, catching them from behind if they tried to circle end, dumping them on the ground if they tried to pass, and challenging the big bruising fullbacks to come through his part of the line. The Packers also took advantage of his speed on offense, sometimes installing a screen pass play that made Cal eligible to receive a pass.

Hubbard played with the Packers from 1929 until 1935, when he was thirty-five years old. He thought his playing days were at an end and he had begun a promising career as a baseball umpire in the minor leagues. But in 1936 he was called out of retirement by an old Giant teammate, Steve Owen, who had become that team's head coach. "I need you, Cal," Owen said. Hubbard, now thirty-six, was indestructible. At the end of the 1936 season, Cal hung up his football cleats for good.

But his name did not vanish from the sports pages, for he became in time as famous in big-league baseball as he had been in football. He became a celebrated umpire in the major leagues. He was a colorful and formidable figure on a baseball field, towering over all ballplayers and incapable of being intimidated by the most ferocious of umpire-baiters. So he remained for almost two decades, acclaimed as the best in the league.

There was no doubt about his name being immortalized in the Professional Football Hall of Fame when that shrine came into being in 1963. He was among the charter seventeen players named.

There were no objectors. After all, no one could argue against perfection. And that's what Robert Calvin Hubbard was in football history — the perfect tackle.

ELROY HIRSCH
"Crazy Legs"

They called him "Crazylegs" when he roamed the big-league pro gridirons in pursuit of his football fame and fortune. But Elroy Hirsch enriched his curious and unique nickname with the glory of a legend — ever to be remembered as pro football's most incredible pass-catching end. No other end in history ever caught forward passes like Crazylegs. He was able to catch long and impossible passes while running at full speed with his head turned back. He could vary his speed, change direction while in full flight, fake, and almost always outmaneuver enemy tacklers. It was practically impossible for enemy defenders to stop him when he was on a rampage for touchdown glory.

Football success did not come easily to Elroy Hirsch, however. Born in Wausau, Wisconsin, of Norwegian-German parentage, he seemed only an average football player when he began playing the game in high school. He barely made the "B" team. But in his senior year at Wausau High, he suddenly blossomed as a halfback, scoring 102 points to lead the Wisconsin Valley Conference. His playing also kindled interest among some college football coaches.

Eventually, at the University of Wisconsin, as a 19-year-old sophomore, he skyrocketed to such stardom that he

achieved All-America rating as a top college halfback.

When the United States became involved in World War II, Hirsch entered the Marine Corps, but surprisingly, he wound up at the University of Michigan, under the V-12 program, playing football there. He achieved an unusual feat in acknowledgment of his abilities as an all-around athlete, becoming the first Michigan man ever to win four varsity letters in one year — football, basketball, baseball and track.

When the war ended, Elroy Hirsch turned to pro football, but made the costliest mistake of his young life which almost destroyed him as a football player. Wanted by the Los Angeles Rams of the National Football League, as well as by the Chicago Rockets of the All America Conference, Elroy Hirsch chose the Rockets to play with, for a salary of only $7,000 a season.

The three seasons he played for the Chicago Rockets were the most miserable of his football career. So inept was that team that it won only seven games in three years. Moreover, in those unhappy years, Hirsch took more than his share of physical punishment as the Rockets' halfback. He tore muscles in his back, and damaged his right knee so severely that he feared he would never run again. But the worst was yet to come. During a game played in 1948, he failed to get up from under a pile of enemy tacklers. He suffered a fractured skull, and spent a long time in a hospital. It was a miracle that he survived that injury. When he was well enough to try to run again, he discovered to his horror that his coordination was gone.

Although he was told never to play football again, Hirsch had the guts and fierce determination to resume playing big-league pro football. Secretly, he undertook a Spartan training program of gymnasium exercises, and though again and again he blacked out and fell on his face, he continued to work out privately. A year later, he returned to pro football to play for the Los Angeles Rams. It was the beginning of a new football career for Elroy Hirsch. He became an end for the Rams, and soon, the scourge of the National Football League. His matchless skills in catching forward passes, with a fearless disregard of the consequences, had never before been seen in the National Football League.

In 1951, he led the Rams to their first pro football championship of the world. In that glorious season, Crazylegs, as Hirsch came to be known (and feared), ran for a record 1,495 yards, a feat that has never been equaled by an end. He also snared 17 touchdown passes while running at full speed with his head flung straight back. That feat also was an all-time record.

Crazylegs starred for the Los Angeles Rams for nine years, and so amazing were his exploits as a pass receiver that he established himself as pro football's most incredible pass-catching end.

Following the 1957 season, Crazylegs Hirsch found that it was no longer much fun catching impossible forward passes and playing big-league pro football, so he retired as a player. He left behind him a record of 343 passes received, for 6,299 yards, and 53 touchdowns.

The legendary "crazy" legs of super-end Elroy Hirsch carried him far up the glory road to football greatness. For he is now enshrined in Pro Football's Hall of Fame as one of the immortals of the game.

EDDIE LeBARON
The Small Giant

Football has always been the big man's sport, particularly in college big time and in the big-league professional ranks. But the story of Eddie LeBaron, a 5-foot-7-inch, 150-pound college wonder who played and starred in the rugged ranks of the big-time pros for eleven seasons, is an inspiring one to any youngster who has been discouraged from playing sports because of his size. It was he who created a glorious saga of a little guy making good in the face of insurmountable obstacles.

LeBaron, an only child, was born in 1917 in San Rafael, California, where his father operated a large dairy ranch. Although he was "a little bit of a squirt," he loved the game of football, and while other small fry played marbles or hide-and-seek, he dreamed of football fame. When only eight years old, tiny Eddie possessed an old helmet, shoulder pads, and a football jersey, and he was always busy throwing long forward passes to his uncle, Jack Sims, a former football star at St. Mary's. By the time he was ten, Eddie could hit a receiver between the eyes at distances up to 50 yards. When the time came for him to go to high school, he was ready for his first bid at football fame. An extremely bright boy, he entered Oakdale High at twelve and became a spectacular football star. In every game pint-sized Eddie rushed for big yardage and threw several touchdown passes.

After being graduated from high school, the prodigy was geared to enter Stanford University at Palo Alto. He nursed a dream of some day quarterbacking for the Indians' football team. But the first time little Eddie met Marchmont Schwartz, the famed Notre Dame All-America who was then head football coach of Stanford, LeBaron was quickly sent on his way.

"Go home and grow up a little before you try out for college football," coach Schwartz said. But LeBaron didn't go home. Instead, he withdrew from Stanford and enrolled at the College of the Pacific, a small school in Stockton, California, where the head coach was the illustrious "Grand Old Man of Football," Amos Alonzo Stagg.

Stagg saw something in the tiny LeBaron. Eddie made the varsity in his freshman year (in those days, freshmen were eligible at some of the smaller schools) and began making headlines. College of the Pacific booked games with important big-name schools, and one of them that year was Northwestern, long famed for its rugged football teams. The game was played at Evanston, Illinois, and when the fans saw LeBaron's size, they hooted derisively. But on the second play of the game, Eddie dashed into his own end zone to intercept a Northwestern pass and flipped the ball laterally to a teammate, who converted the daring play into a 101-yard touchdown. Later in the game, Eddie threw a touchdown pass, and Northwestern, which had expected a rout, had to settle for a 26-13 victory. Little LeBaron got all the headlines as the hero of that game.

That's the way it was during Eddie's entire glorious college career. At first sight of Eddie, the rival team would hoot, but the sneers would change to awe once the little back got hold of a football. LeBaron was an exceptionally gifted ball-handler. He originated what is known as the "belly series," in which he would thrust the ball into the stomach of a halfback or fullback and then run with him a few steps. Then he would take back the ball and run with it, or pass, or let the other back take it. His faking was so remarkable that the other team was bewildered as often as not.

Eddie was mentioned on many All-America teams, so when he graduated, the pro teams of the National Football League knew about him. He was drafted by the Washington Redskins. And so began LeBaron's eleven-year stretch in the big leagues of pro football.

In the 1950 All-Star game at Chicago, LeBaron quarterbacked the collegians when they upset the favored Philadelphia Eagles, 17-7. Eddie had the Eagles running around in circles while he faked, ran, and passed. But LeBaron's debut as a pro player had to wait for two years while he served with the Marines at Korea. He was injured in action and won a battlefield decoration for bravery.

"Little Eddie was the most fearless soldier I've ever seen," said a veteran army officer of that war.

When Eddie reported to the Redskins in 1952, Sammy Baugh, football's fabulous forward passer, was in his final season. Impatient for immediate pro grid action, Eddie went off to the Canadian pro league to spend a season playing for the Calgary Stampeders. But when he returned to the National Football League, the Redskin quarterback job was his. He quickly became a puzzle as well as a sensation. Because of his small size, he had to throw passes in a different way from all the other pro quarterbacks. While they could throw a football with speed, little Eddie had to loft the ball high over the heads of the giants who made up the opposing line. They used to say that he threw only "pop flies" to his receivers, but he was incomparable at it.

Other teams had doubts that the amazing "little squirt" could throw the "long ball," but early in his pro career he shattered those doubts by throwing four touchdown passes, each of them better than 35 yards, against the then champion New York Giants. In 1958, LeBaron led the National Football League in passing, and he was voted the Most Valuable Player of the Washington Redskins.

The incredible runt who never was supposed to make it big in big-league pro ball was also making good elsewhere. In the off-seasons he went to law school, and he earned his degree as an attorney-at-law. When the Washington Redskins traded him to the new Dallas Cowboys in 1960, Eddie LeBaron intended to quit football and practice law, but he was persuaded to change his mind and play four more seasons, until he finally quit in 1963 at the age of thirty-six.

Football fans never quite got over his amazing gridiron exploits, despite his size. Once he was asked, "How good a quarterback do you think you would have been if you had been six inches taller?" Eddie's reply was direct and simple: "I don't know. I've never been any taller."

He spelled out an inspiring and heart-warming story of a little guy with courage and determination making good in the roughest of professional games. In the face of great odds, Eddie LeBaron was the mightiest football mite of them all.

LOU GROZA
"The Toe"

In 1946, when Lou Groza, age twenty-two, first came to play in the violent world of big-league professional football, he had no college background for his gridiron fame. Not even once had he ever played in a collegiate football game.

Born in Berea, Ohio, in 1924, Groza attended his home-town high school with no athletic distinction. When he enrolled as a student at Ohio State University in Columbus, he didn't even complete his freshman year, leaving college to enlist in the United States Army. In 1946, when he was discharged from military service, instead of returning to college, Lou Groza decided to take a whirl at professional football for his fame and fortune. Paul Brown, the famous football coach of the Cleveland Browns, in the newly formed All-America Conference, hired him to play tackle for his team.

The burly Lou Groza quickly proved himself to be a most unusual, aggressive and rugged offensive tackle of brutal effectiveness. He soon also revealed himself to be an unusually talented kicker of footballs. When he applied his toe to a football, he punted with astonishing power and surprising accuracy. So, he became the kicking specialist of the Cleveland Browns.

But Lou Groza became even more than that. His amazing accuracy in kicking long field goals changed the whole concept of pro football play. It was Groza who first proved that a football team with a strong and effective field-goal kicker could always be a scoring threat from midfield or even in its own territory.

In the four seasons the Cleveland Browns were the invincible champions of the All-America Conference, before that football league collapsed and went out of existence, Lou Groza scored 259 points for his team — with his toe.

It was when the Cleveland Browns joined the National Football League in 1950 that Lou Groza began to establish himself as the most amazing kicking specialist in all pro football history. So incredible and awesome were his punting feats that throughout the football world he came to be known simply as "The Toe."

He became the first player to score as many as a thousand points with his toe. Also, he became the first kicker in pro football to score in as many as 107 consecutive games. Over a fourteen-year period in the NFL, his magic toe accounted for at least 80 points per season. In the seventeen years he starred in the National Football League, he kicked 234 field goals from all distances, and 641 extra points after touchdowns. And while he was accomplishing all that as a kicker, so effective a tackle was he for the Cleveland Browns that six times he was chosen

as an offensive tackle on the All-NFL first team.

Lou Groza, who had never played any college football for his fame, was forty-three years old when he finally quit playing big-league pro football. By that time he had become a gridiron legend. His credentials were matchless. In his fabulous twenty-one-year career in pro football, over a stretch of 268 games, he had kicked 264 field goals and 810 extra points after touchdowns for an astounding total of 1,608 points.

The wonder of Lou Groza as football's outstanding kicking specialist transcends the many awesome statistics which his super-toe wrote into the record books. He paved the way and set the pace for all the phenomenal punting marvels in pro football history.

PAUL LEROY ROBESON
The Hall of Fame Outcast

In more than a century of football history, many blacks have played the game for gridiron glory, and a host of them have gained imperishable fame. But no black gridiron-great ever lived so fabulous and fantastic a career as did Paul Robeson. His saga of glory found and lost is unique, and will continue to haunt football memory through the ages.

Born in Princeton, New Jersey, in 1898, Paul Robeson was the son of a runaway Negro slave who became a minister. From boyhood, he revealed himself as a most unusual versatile athlete. Upon his graduation from high school, he was so well-known as a schoolboy football player that in 1915, Rutgers University awarded him an athletic scholarship. He was the first black to attend that private school for higher education, which was notable as the college that won the first intercollegiate football game played in America.

At Rutgers, Paul Robeson became a most magnificent athlete for collegiate fame. He earned thirteen varsity letters in four sports. In addition, he was a brilliant student. He won membership in the Phi Beta Kappa honorary scholastic society, he was an outstanding debater, and in his senior year he was class valedictorian.

Still, his most famous achievements at Rutgers were on the gridiron. A huge, agile, and swift-footed football player,

6-foot-3-inches tall and 217 pounds heavy, he played end for the Rutgers team and became the most glamorous college football player of his time.

Equally adept at offense and defense while playing sixty minutes of every game, strong-armed Robeson was a genuis at catching forward passes. His spectacular touchdown-runs often spelled victory for his team. No other black college football-great ever won the national acclaim that Paul Robeson did as Rutgers' gridiron hero.

Twice, in 1917 and 1918, the legendary Walter Camp, father of American football, honored Robeson by naming him All-American end on his annual mythical football team, composed only of the greatest college players of that era. So stirred was Walter Camp by Paul Robeson's playing that he declared publicly: "There never had been a more serviceable end in football, both on offense and defense, than Paul Robeson. The game of college football will never know a greater end."

When his college years were over, Robeson turned briefly to professional football to earn tuition money he needed at Columbia Law School. No sooner did he gain his law degree than he quit playing pro football. But instead of practicing law for his fame and fortune, he turned to the legitimate stage and became one of America's most noted actors. He also starred on the motion picture screen.

But that wasn't enough glory and fame for Paul Robeson. He also turned to the concert stage, and became one of the world's most famous singers. His golden voice was heard in song by millions of people throughout the world.

Even that wasn't enough achievement for that incredible one-time All-American football immortal. He also became the first famous militant black in America to fight for equality for the members of his race. It not only made him a controversial political figure, but it earned him the ugly hostility of a legion of bigots.

Discouraged by the vilification and humiliations encountered at every turn, Paul Robeson went to Europe, where he worked and lived for many years. When he finally returned to his native land, he was almost completely forgotten as the one-time fabulous All-American football wonder. He learned that a great injustice had been committed against him by the ruling powers of the college football world. He was an outcast from the National Football Hall of Fame where dwell all college gridiron immortals.

To this day, Paul Robeson, one of the greatest of college football players in history, is the only two-time All-American player who has been denied official enshrinement in the Football Hall of Fame, even though he is an authentic immortal of the game.

JERRY KRAMER
A Winner Never Quits

That Jerry Kramer ever became an outstanding football player was a miracle. He survived enough physical misfortunes to kill him several times over — the most accident-prone football player who ever achieved gridiron greatness.

Born on a farm in Jordan, Montana, Jerry was a mere five years old when he suffered the pain of his first physical misfortune. He tried to chop some wood with a heavy axe, and as he lifted it over his head, it slipped from his grasp, plummeting downward, The sharp blade slashed his chin and neck. He was rushed to a hospital where doctors worked for hours to save his life. It was Jerry's first demonstration of an amazing talent for survival.

He was twelve when he suffered a second painful misfortune. He fell out of a tree, severely injuring his arm and back. Again he survived, and by the age of sixteen, he was a husky, broad-shouldered, muscular lad who loved football. He had become a star tackle for the Sand Point High School football team, in Sand Point, Idaho, where his family had moved some years before.

His next injury happened in manual arts class when he accidentally backed into a wood-working lathe that tore away a large hunk of flesh and ripped his hip muscle. Nevertheless, he was soon back playing football for his school team.

One day, soon after, Jerry went bird-hunting with his grandfather's old double-barreled shotgun. It discharged accidentally, and Jerry fell wounded in the right arm and side. He was rushed to a hospital, where doctors worked frantically over him. Half the muscle of his right forearm had been destroyed, and both bones below the elbow were fractured. The ulnar nerve in his wrist was also crushed, and some of the pellets had penetrated his side, puncturing his liver. Moreover, he had lost a vast quantity of blood.

Jerry Kramer hovered between life and death for weeks. It was a miracle that he survived after several delicate operations. He left the hospital with a right arm scarred and rutted for the rest of his life. After that near-fatal accident, Jerry resumed his football playing, but disaster struck the youngster again. One day, while running to catch a frisky calf, Jerry tripped over a rotted board. A large jagged fragment pierced deep into his leg and groin. Again he returned to a hospital for more surgery to save his life. Again he survived. And three weeks later, courageous Jerry was back on the football field, playing for his school team so well that he gained fame as an All-State tackle.

Upon graduating from Sand Point High, Jerry was awarded an athletic scholarship, for his football skills, to the

University of Idaho. He almost failed to begin his college gridiron career because of another near-fatal accident. The car in which he was riding drove off the road into a ditch and burst into flames. Miraculously, Jerry Kramer walked away from that disaster without a scratch.

At Idaho University, Jerry gained fame as an outstanding college lineman and kicker. He was a magnificent guard on offense and defense, acclaimed as one of the finest ever seen in intercollegiate gridiron competition. But the injury-jinx still pursued him. He sustained a neck injury and developed a chipped vertebra which required more surgery.

When his glorious college football days were over, 6-foot-3-inch, 235-pound, accident-prone Jerry Kramer came to the violent world of big-league professional football to play for the Green Bay Packers of the National Football League. His rookie year in pro football in 1958 was a most painful indoctrination. As a guard, courageous Jerry played against some of the roughest, meanest, cruelest, and cleverest opponents in the game. He absorbed many scars, both physical and mental. But he didn't quit, because his guts and will to survive were matchless.

He learned his pro grid lessons so quickly and well that he was hailed as one of the greatest guards in the game only a season later. Agile and powerful, with clever moves, Jerry became a devastating blocker, and his skills and adroitness in leading running plays through enemy defenses made him a key spark plug on the Green Bay Packer team that went on to unforgettable triumphs. Kramer also became the Packers' outstanding kicker. One season he set a team record with 16 field goals and 43 extra points for a total of 91 points.

But he still was the most accident-prone football player in the game. Over the seasons, he suffered a detached retina of his right eye, forcing him to undergo a delicate operation to save his sight. He also suffered a severe fracture of the tibia, the main bone in the leg which became separated from his ankle. Even though doctors predicted that his football career was over, heroic Jerry Kramer did not quit. He came back to play pro football, even though he had a bolt in his injured ankle to hold the bone in his broken leg in place.

Neither accident nor injury ever stopped Jerry Kramer from playing superior football. In less than a year, he underwent eight corrective operations. By the time he was 29 years old, he had had 23 operations, with more than 500 stitches sewn into his wounded body. He was actually so close to death once that a shocked football world was informed that he had died on an operating table. But just when his legion of stunned admirers began to plan his funeral, Jerry Kramer surprised them again with his amazing talent for survival. Always he came back from his misfortunes with his full quota of guts and courage to enrich his fame as one of the greatest football players in history.

For all of twelve years, he remained one of the mightiest offensive guards in pro football, and so magnificent and vital was his playing that he was the key element in the Green Bay Packers' triumphal glory march to six conference title victories and five National Football League championships. He also helped the Packers win the first two Super Bowl classics.

Finally, at the age of 32, after he had helped the Packers win another world pro football championship, Jerry Kramer quit playing football. He left the game a winner, ever to be remembered as one of the greatest guards in football history. But he also left the game with a unique distinction. Upon his departure he was acclaimed by all as the most courageous and heroic athlete who had ever played college and pro football. As the most accident-prone football player in history, he was proof that a winner never quits.

BOB WATERFIELD
Doing Everything Was His Specialty

Bob Waterfield, quarterback of the Cleveland and Los Angeles Rams for eight years, was undoubtedly the most versatile man ever to play that position. Besides being a brilliant field general, a superior passer and a surprisingly adept runner, he punted as well as anybody in the league. Three times he was the foremost field-goal kicker. No one did so many things on a football field so well.

He led the Rams to three consecutive Western Conference titles in Los Angeles, and, in 1945, as a rookie, he brought the championship to Cleveland before that club was moved to the Coast. He made All-Pro in his first year in the pros, and also was named Most Valuable Player, the first time ever that the award was won by a first-year man.

Waterfield was born in Elmira, New York, in 1920, but his family moved to Van Nuys, California, when he was a youngster. At Van Nuys High School, he made no blazing marks on the athletic fields — he weighed less than 150 pounds. Then he worked in an aircraft factory, playing football on the side, earning enough money to enter the University of California at Los Angeles in 1940.

His football talent came to the fore then, and within a year he was first-string quarterback for an impressive UCLA team, which won its conference title and went to the Rose Bowl.

In 1943, he enlisted in the Army and was sent to Officers Candidate School at Fort Benning, Georgia, but he injured a knee and received a medical discharge. He went back to UCLA and picked up where he left off. He was drafted by the Cleveland Rams.

That was when he had his sensational rookie year, climaxed by the Rams' defeat of the Washington Redskins in the title game, 15-14, with Waterfield throwing two touchdown passes and completing 14 of 27 aerials.

After the 1945 season, the Cleveland franchise was moved to Los Angeles, where Waterfield and the Rams chalked up three straight division titles. His amazing versatility as a field general, passer, runner and kicker contributed heavily to all three title triumphs.

Waterfield introduced, among other things, the "home-run" pass, something pro teams had used with great reluctance before he came into the limelight. Often, on third-and-six situations, Bob would fade back and loft 40- and 50-yard passes, which often caught the opposing backs off guard. Today, of course, the "bomb" forward pass ball is a standard operating maneuver for most pro teams.

During his illustrious eight-year pro career, he threw 1,618 forward passes, completing 814, for 11,893 yards, and 99 touchdowns. His punting was even more spectacular. Again and again, he booted 88-yard punts, and his 315 career punts totaled 13,382 yards.

It was in a game played in 1951, against the powerful and favored Detroit Lions, in a contest to decide the Western Division league championship, when Waterfield astonished a crowd of more than 80,000 spectators by giving the most amazing and greatest punting performance ever before seen in major-league pro football. He booted five field goals from all distances to become the first player in National Football League history to kick five field goals in a single game.

In 1952, when Bob Waterfield retired as a big-league football player, his fame as the most versatile of all quarterbacks was by then solidly assured for posterity. He was enshrined in the Professional Football Hall of Fame as one of the game's most honored immortals.

WILBUR ("PETE") HENRY
They Called Him "Fats"

Perhaps the greatest tackle the pro game ever saw — when tackles still played both offense and defense — was a round, jolly man who carried 250 pounds on a six-foot frame, yet who moved with the grace of a ballet dancer in bringing down ball-carriers or in leading a blocking phalanx.

He was Wilbur ("Pete") Henry, also known as "Fats," a rough-and-tumble performer in the early days of pro ball, who was described by old-timers as a "good-natured terror who could take out the entire side of an opposing line."

Fats was born in Mansfield, Ohio, in 1897. In high school he was a bruising fullback, but when he tried out for the team at Washington and Jefferson College in Pennsylvania, the coach switched the 215-pound youngster to tackle. From then on, Henry's exploits in the line were memorable, and he was named All-America at the position and, later, all-time All-America.

He turned professional in 1920, signing with the Canton Bulldogs coached by Jim Thorpe. It was only the second year of the fledgling National Football League. Henry played with Canton for six seasons, and in two of those years the club was undefeated. Henry became All-Pro for three seasons, then moved to the championship New York Giants for the 1927 season, and to the Pottsville

Maroons, then in the NFL, in 1928.

Henry, over the years, made plays which sounded unbelievable. One time, he broke through the line to try to block a punt (one of his specialties), and as the kicker dropped the ball and brought back his foot, the speedy Henry plucked the ball in midair, tucked it under his arm and ran for a touchdown.

Another time, he blocked a punt, recovered it quickly, and ran for a touchdown and converted the extra point. Then he kicked two field goals for a 13-0 victory.

That kicking faculty became Fats Henry's specialty in his later years. Sometimes, in practice, he could kick the length of the field. And he still has an entry in the record book: "Longest Punt, 94 yards, Wilbur Henry, Canton vs. Akron, October 28, 1923." For many years he also held the NFL record for a 52-yard drop kick for Canton against Akron.

Later, Fats became athletic director at his old college, Washington and Jefferson, and he died in 1952. He thus never knew that he was honored by being elected to the Professional Hall of Fame some years later.

But it is likely that he knew that he was an extraordinary player. The attitudes of the linemen he played against would have told him that.

YELBERTON ABRAHAM TITTLE
The Baldest Man In the Game

Of all the fabulous quarterbacks known, perhaps the most appealing and possibly the most heroic was Y. A. Tittle, the baldest man who ever played big-league professional football.

Born in Marshall, Texas, he began throwing forward passes in his boyhood. By the time he graduated from Marshall High School, he was an outstanding schoolboy quarterback, good enough to win a scholarship to Louisiana State University.

In 1944, as a freshman in college, he began playing varsity football. By the time he was a senior, Y. A. Tittle was a well-known college gridiron star, not only of regional but of national scope.

In 1949, he began his major pro football career with the Baltimore Colts, then in the All-American Football Conference. But after starring for them for three seasons, he was traded to the San Francisco 49ers of the National Football League. There, quarterback Tittle played for ten years, even though through the seasons he was an unfortunate victim of a brain concussion, a collapsed lung, knee injuries, smashed ribs, a broken cheekbone, a broken wrist, a broken toe, amnesia and asthma. Nevertheless, his gridiron ex-

ploits established him as one of the gamest and best quarterbacks extant.

Cool, crisp and wise in gridiron battle, Y. A. Tittle was often hailed as the number one passer in the game. One of the quickest and surest ways to a touchdown score at that time was to have baldheaded Y. A. Tittle do the pitching. Football never had a more accurate passer, and often he unleashed astonishing forward passes when least expected. A wrist thrower, Tittle pitched winning forward passes in the most unpredictable ways — sidearm, overhand, and even underhand. Enemy defenders never knew where his short and long passes came from.

But when baldheaded Y. A. Tittle had aged to thirty-five and was sidelined by a serious knee injury, the San Francisco 49ers came to believe that their star quarterback had grown too old and used-up as a big-time pro player. And so, prior to the start of the 1961 season, they traded him to the New York Giants, who at that time were desperately in need of a quarterback. The Giants' followers scoffed at the "ridiculous" acquisition which had brought a washed-up, old, baldheaded quarterback to the New York football club.

A miracle happened, however, when Y. A. Tittle put on a Giants' football uniform. He suddenly rediscovered his youth, and he embarked on a second brilliant career in the pro ranks as a quarterback-great. The baldest player in the game transformed the New York Giants into a powerful winning football team, featuring the best pass offense in big-league pro football. With superior field generalship, magnificent forward passing, and inspiring leadership, quar-

terback Tittle led the Giants to three consecutive National Football League championship playoffs (1961, 1962, and 1963).

In those glorious three seasons, Y. A. Tittle once again became the most brilliant quarterback in the pro game. His feats were astonishing. Once, he pegged fifty passes in one game. Another time, he passed for seven touchdowns, and completed 27 passes out of 39 — 12 in a row — for 505 yards. In the 1963 season, that baldheaded veteran of two pro teams, with more than 13 playing years behind him, was at his glittering best. He attempted 367 passes, and completed 221 for 3,145 yards and 36 touchdowns.

Though he was no ball-carrier, quarterback Tittle often would crash into an enemy line or dive headfirst over an opposing line, if that was the only way to gain yardage or score. His spectacular quarterbacking not only found him renewed glory, but also made the New York Giants the most glamorous of teams.

He was thirty-eight years old when he finally came to the end of the glory road. A rival player tackled him so viciously that he almost twisted his leg off. Y. A. Tittle limped off the field. Before the start of the 1965 season, he announced his retirement as a player.

He left behind a shining record as one of the greatest quarterbacks pro football ever had. He had given 17 years to the game. He had attempted 4,395 forward passes, and had completed 2,427 for 33,070 yards, and 242 touchdowns.

It was no surprise when Y. A. Tittle, the baldest man who ever played big-league pro football, was enshrined in the National Pro Football Hall of Fame as an immortal of the game.

EMLEN TUNNELL
He Was the First

One of the greatest defensive players in the history of big-league professional football was Emlen Tunnell, who one day in 1948 strolled into the camp of the New York Giants, uninvited and little-known, asking for a job as a football player. That 6-foot-1-inch, 190-pound prospect persuaded the dubious Giants to hire him for a season's salary of $5,000. It was one of football's greatest bargains. Emlen Tunnell starred in the National Football League for fourteen glorious seasons as the game's premier runback artist and pass interceptor. One season (1952) he accounted for 924 yards gained on the defense, while the league's leading rusher that year, Dan Towler of the Los Angeles Rams, totaled only 890 yards. It was the only time in NFL history that a defensive back leader outgained the offensive leader over a full season of pro play.

Oddly enough, when Tunnell joined the New York Giants to begin his NFL career, there was a question of whether he would play offense or defense. But no sooner had Tunnell joined the defensive unit than he began to set innumerable records for his fame as the most feared runback marvel in the league. One season he established a new record with 38 punt returns — and once, in a single game, he performed the astonishing feat of returning eight punts.

Tunnell's road to football heroism was a rocky one. He was born in Garrett Hill, a suburb of Philadelphia, in 1922, and his high school athletic skills earned him a scholarship to Toledo College. As a freshman, he came out of a scrimmage with a broken neck and was told that he could never play football again. That injury did not keep him from joining the Coast Guard in World War II, and he survived two torpedo attacks on his ship. After his service, he entered the University of Iowa.

He was a tailback in those days, and he played for two years before looking around for a professional job. He got one with the New York Giants in 1948, played with them for eleven years, and topped that with three more years playing for the Green Bay Packers. Over one stretch, he played in 158 consecutive games, a remarkable feat in the grueling world of major-league professional football.

Tunnell also established records for later players to shoot at. He had the most interceptions (79), the most yards returned with interceptions (1,282), most punt returns (258), and most yards gained returning punts (2,209).

After his first disappointment at not playing offense, Emlen began getting a charge from his defensive work. As a key man in the Giants' famed "umbrella defense," in the early Fifties, Tunnell made NFL quarterbacks sit up and take notice. One year the invincible Cleveland Browns came to town and the Giants bottled their attack so effectively that the Giants shut them out for the first time in history. Tunnell was in the middle of most of the brilliant defensive moves.

The Giants won the NFL title in 1956 by steamrollering the Chicago Bears, 47-7, and Tunnell was credited again with defensive genius. In 1958 he was on the team that won the Eastern Conference title, but lost to the Baltimore Colts in the playoff game.

When he finally left the New York Giants to play for fabulous coach Vince Lombardi and his Green Bay Packers, Emlen Tunnell performed so tenaciously, efficiently and brilliantly that the Packers captured two division titles in a row (1960 and 1961), curiously defeating the Giants in the latter year to win the pro football championship of the world.

There never was a doubt that Emlen Tunnell would be ushered into the National Professional Football Hall of Fame for gridiron immortality. He was enshrined in 1967. When it happened, he was so humble and grateful for the coveted honor bestowed upon him so soon after his playing days were over that he called the Director of the famed football shrine and thanked him.

"Don't thank me," Emlen Tunnell was told. "You did it all yourself!"

But the greatest honor for his unforgettable football greatness came to Emlen Tunnell in 1965 when he returned to his beloved New York Giants to become a defensive coach. He thereby became the first fulltime Negro coach ever in the National Football League.

ELMER KENNETH STRONG
Local Boy Makes Good

No kicker in football history ever had more powerful leg drive than Ken Strong. That gift blazed the trail for him to his gridiron immortality.

When Ken Strong first began to gain fame as a most unusual football hero, however, he was more than merely a great kicker. In the late Twenties, when he was starring for New York University, he was being hailed as the greatest running halfback in college football. He ran all over the biggest and most powerful college football teams of his time. Smashing into enemy lines with crushing power, throwing passes, tackling and blocking all over the field, that 6-foot-1-inch, 200-pound Violet halfback also kicked fifty-yard punts with ease, and frequently his booming pre-game eighty-yard drop kicks psyched out the opposition before the start of important football games. When All-American Ken Strong was making collegiate football history for his fame, the Violets of NYU were equal to the outstanding and best college football teams in the nation.

In 1928, Strong climaxed his illustrious college football career with a spectacular season. He gained 3,800 yards to set a collegiate record, and he led the nation's scorers with 153 points.

Naturally, when glamorous Ken Strong was done with his college football days, the New York Giants of the National

Football League anxiously wanted that spectacular local football hero for their team. To persuade him to turn pro, they were willing to offer him $4,000 a season, a reasonable figure for a big-league pro player in those days. But they lost him

because the club official the Giants sent to sign Ken Strong was foolishly tightfisted. He believed that he could snare that fabulous college halfback, who could do everything, for a salary of only $3,000 a season. Ken Strong quickly rejected that offer, and instead of becoming a Giant, he signed with the Stapleton Stapes, a Staten Island club, then a member of the National Football League. He starred for the Stapletons for four seasons, until that pro football club folded in 1932.

When that happened, the New York Giants finally acquired Ken Strong as a player. Strong was just what the Giants needed to become a winning team. Running with hammering power, throwing passes or receiving them, punting 75 yards, or kicking 50-yard field goals, halfback Ken Strong was a Giant with an inspiring spirit for his teammates. He sparked the Giants to an Eastern Division crown in his first season. The following year (1934) he led them to the National Football League title and the pro football championship of the world.

As the seasons passed, All-Pro Ken Strong, more and more, gained renown as pro football's greatest kicker. His power punts produced many winning field goals for the Giants. Still, at the peak of his fame as a matchless kicker, Strong's salary was no more than $6,000 a season.

So, when the new American Football League was organized, Ken Strong deserted the Giants and jumped to the new league. The National Football League regarded Ken Strong's abandonment of the Giants' team such an unpardonable act of disloyalty that he was suspended from the NFL for five years.

In 1938, however, the Giants invited Ken Strong to return and play for their team. He did, and he had a magnificent season, before he decided to retire from pro football.

But football glory still beckoned to Ken Strong. During World War II, when he was thirty-seven years old, the Giants, desperately in need of a top kicker, persuaded Strong to return to the game. Again, his kicking was phenomenal. In 1944, he led the NFL in field goals. He continued to play for the New York Giants until he was forty-one years old.

During his nine seasons with the Giants, he scored 351 points, which stood as a team record for years. At one time, he also held the club records for the longest field goal, most extra points kicked, most consecutive extra points kicked, and most points scored in one season with the foot. He also scored another 175 points with his toe while playing for the other pro teams.

With all the punting Ken Strong did during his fabulous years as a big-league pro football player, he not only carved his fame into football history as a great kicker with the most powerful leg drive ever seen, but he also booted his way into the Professional Football Hall of Fame, ever to be honored as an immortal of the game.

GALE SAYERS
Rookie In a Hurry

In 1964, his rookie season with the Chicago Bears, Gale Sayers, a six-foot-one-inch, 200-pound halfback, scored more touchdowns (twenty-two) than any other player in the history of the National Football League. Also, he tied the all-time record for most touchdowns in one game (six), and was acclaimed the equal of football's most notable luminaries. In more than half-a-century of professional football, no other first-year man ever had made such a spectacular and devastating debut.

The "Kansas Comet," as Gale Sayers was known, started off his initial season in the big-league pro ranks with such a flourish that, after playing only a few games, he was being acclaimed as

"Rookie of the Year." But it was late in his first season when rookie Sayers staged the greatest exhibition ever seen in a big-time pro football game, starring a grid newcomer.

The Chicago Bears took on the San Francisco Forty-Niners before a crowd of 65,000. The first time the Bears had the ball, they started from their 20-yard line. Rookie Sayers caught a screen pass, shook off all tacklers, and ran 80 yards for a touchdown. Next, he skirted end on a 21-yard spurt for another touchdown. Then he took a pitchout from his quarterback to race for a third touchdown. He added another touchdown with a spectacular 50-yard dash, and still another touchdown with a furious plunge through the Forty-Niners' line. But he still was not yet done with glory for that game. Sayers caught San Francisco's kick on his own 15-yard line, ran straight upfield, swerved away from tacklers, then scurried crosswise through enemy defenders, and found the daylight he needed to complete an 85-yard punt-return for his sixth touchdown of that game. When it ended, the shy, retiring Gale Sayers showed extreme modesty.

"I'm just beginning to learn how to play pro football," he told the surprised reporters who had flocked around him for post-game interviews.

Gale Sayers, however, was no novice at performing the unusual and incredible in football play. Born in Wichita, Kansas, on May 30, 1943, the son of a automobile-repair shopkeeper, he began winning grid fame while still at Omaha Central High School. He was an All-State halfback, and so widespread was his schoolboy football fame that many colleges offered him tempting athletic scholarships. He chose the University of Kan-

sas, where he would become its greatest football star. In three collegiate football seasons, All-American Gale Sayers rushed for 2,675 yards (an average of 7 yards per carry) and he set several all-time Jayhawk records, like a 99-yard touchdown run from scrimmage, and gaining 283 yards rushing in a single game. In 1964, when the Chicago Bears snared him for pro football, Gale Sayers received more than $150,000.

From a phenomenal rookie-wonder, the "Kansas Comet" quickly grew into a full-fledged pro grid-great. As the football seasons passed, he performed amazing feats, scoring touchdowns in a surprising variety of ways. He set an awesome pace on the glory road leading toward the peaks of pro-football greatness. A long and glorious career was predicted for Gale Sayers as a natural for Hall of Fame immortality.

But a cruel fate intervened. After only seven seasons in the pro ranks, a series of severe knee injuries finally forced Gale Sayers to quit playing big-league football for his fame and fortune. He was only twenty-eight at the time. It was a sad finish for the saga of the Kansas Comet.

But by then, Gale Sayers already had impressive credentials to give permanent fame to his name as one of football's greatest halfbacks. In the sixty-six pro games he had played, he had rushed for 4,918 yards, galloped to 56 touchdowns, and scored 336 points.

What will be remembered most of Gale Sayers as a genuine gridiron-great is that he was the most incredible and most spectacular rookie in the history of big-time professional football.

It isn't likely that any other football player will ever eclipse the glory of Gale Sayers as a rookie in a hurry for fame.

GEORGE HALAS
Mr. National Football League

For more than half a century, George Stanley Halas devoted his life to football as player, coach, innovator and owner — and his contributions were so masterful that he changed the whole face of the game. He was known as "Mr. NFL," but his influence was greater than that. It touched every professional, sandlot, high school and college team in the country.

When he furbished the T-formation to the point where his Chicago Bears ran roughshod over their pro opponents, everybody else switched to the T, too, and from there evolved all of the latter-day formations now seen on football fields everywhere in the land.

Halas was born in Chicago, Illinois, on February 2, 1895, youngest child in a family of seven. His father and mother both had come to this country from Prague, Czechoslovakia, and took a dim view of their sons' interest in sports. They wanted doctors and lawyers.

But George persisted and became a tackle in high school, even though he weighed only 140 pounds, and at the University of Illinois he tried out as halfback. He made up in aggressiveness what he lacked in physical stature, and he caught the eye of the coach, who said: "He runs so hard, he is likely to kill himself. Better make him an end." So he played end at Illinois, captained the basketball team,

and was an outstanding outfielder in baseball, so good that he later had a tryout with the New York Yankees.

Football was his first love, though, and during World War I, as an ensign at the Great Lakes Naval Training Station, he played well enough to be named on the All-America team.

After he was discharged from the Navy, Halas became enamored of professional football, since an injury had cut short his baseball career. At Decatur, Illinois, a sports enthusiast named A. E. Staley, owner of a corn products company who wanted his firm represented in sports, hired George to head his company's athletic program, including the organization of a football team. Halas did so with vigor, recruiting top-flight players, lured by offers of year-round jobs, as well as two hours off a day for football practice.

In the meanwhile, Halas and a handful of coaches and owners were organizing the American Professional Football Association, which was to become the National Football League. And Halas's sponsor, Staley, suggested that the team be moved from Decatur to Chicago. He gave George a check for $5,000 to help with expenses, but with the understanding that the name Staley be retained for a year.

Eventually, the name of his team was changed to the Chicago Bears, because they played their home games in Wrigley Field, the home of the major-league Chicago Cubs baseball club. Almost immediately, the Bears became winners. In 1921, the team won the then imaginary league championship with a record of ten victories and one loss.

Four years later, Halas gave the then

stagnant and little-popular game of big-league football its biggest and most sensational push to undreamed glory and untold riches. He persuaded the greatest and most glamorous college football player of that time, the immortal super-back, Red Grange, from the University of Illinois, to become a pro player with the Chicago Bears. With hardly a month left of that 1925 pro season, George Halas took Red Grange and his Chicago Bears on an unbelievable barnstorming tour — to play seven games, in seven different cities, in the space of only nine days. His entire football squad consisted of only 18 players. It was a pro football endurance record that will never be equaled. Large crowds saw George Halas's Bears play everywhere. The hectic barnstorming tour came to an end in New York, in a game against the Giants, with a record crowd of more than 80,000 fans present to see that contest. The unprecedented George Halas barnstorming tour with the Chicago Bears and the fabulous Red Grange was the turning point in establishing the big-league pro game as a legitimate and popular sport in the public mind. It helped set up pro football into the game it is today for millions of people.

In 1933, the NFL split into Eastern and Western Divisions. The Bears, coached by owner Halas, won their division in the first two years, winning the playoff game once and losing once. In 1934, the Bears raced through an entire league season of thirteen games without suffering a defeat, a feat accomplished by only two other teams, the Bears of 1942 and the Miami Dolphins of 1972.

The 1940 Halas team was the memorable one that polished up the T-formation which led to such widespread reaction. Though the T had dated back to the turn of the century, it had all but been discarded by 1940 in favor of single- and double-wing formations and Notre Dame's box formation, all designed to spread out the defense. But Halas brought in a man in motion, forcing a defender to cover him, which set up counterplays to confuse the opposition. It worked so well for the glory-hungry Bears that year, that when they came to the final big game for the NFL title against the powerful Washington Redskins, they won the pro football championship of the world by an historic score — 73-0. It was the greatest victory ever scored by a major-league pro football team. For owner-coach George Halas it was the biggest thrill of his lifetime.

George Halas made the Bears the first professional team to hold daily practice sessions. His football team was the first in pro history to travel for games, coast to coast. The Bears were the first pro team to use a band to entertain spectators and have a song of their own (*Bear Down, Chicago Bears*), their own club newspaper, and their games broadcast on radio. George Halas was the first in pro football to utilize films of opponents' games for study. All these innovations for pro football were created by George Halas.

Throughout the years, Halas, owner and coach, was a familiar figure to National Football League fans. He roamed the sidelines, wearing his old brown business suit and a battered fedora, chirping at officials as he followed the play on the field. For about half a century, George Halas dominated pro football. His Chicago Bears won the most championships (7), they won the most games (over 400), and scored the most points (about 12,000). They also scored the most touchdowns (about 1,750) and played before the largest total number of football fans (almost 20 million).

It was a sad day when George Halas finally was forced to quit coaching his Chicago Bears because arthritis kept him from moving about in the fashion he was used to for half a century.

From the very beginning, he was a vital part of big-league professional football. It was said of him, "George Halas may not have invented the pro brand of football — it just seems that way!"

RAYMOND BERRY
The Self-Made Immortal

If there ever was a self-made immortal in football, he was Raymond Berry of Texas.

In high school, he didn't make the team until his senior year. At Southern Methodist University, he failed to win his varsity letter in football until the end of his junior year. In his entire college career as an end, he caught only 33 passes for just one touchdown. Nevertheless, unspectacular a football player as he was, Raymond Berry was fortunate enough to squeeze himself into big-league professional football for the 1955 season when the Baltimore Colts of the National Football League drafted him 20th. No one expected the unheralded rookie to remain in pro football beyond a single season.

But the 6-foot-2-inch, 187-pound Berry, who was neither big nor fast, and who seemingly lacked the skills considered essential for an efficient pass receiver in the pro game, had a fierce determination to make a name for himself in football's big-time. So he hustled and worked harder than any pro rookie ever had done to propel himself to greatness as an end and forward-pass catcher.

For every pass caught in a game, he caught about a thousand in practice. He practiced incessantly until he developed an astonishing repertoire of moves and patterns that made him a pass receiver

no enemy defense could adequately cover. By actual count, he developed 88 maneuvers for getting around enemy defenses in order to catch forward passes thrown to him. Every day Raymond Berry practiced all 88 moves. At home he practiced pass-catching by having his wife throw passes to him.

His most spectacular performance for his ever-growing fame as a pass receiver was in the historic 1958 NFL championship playoff game between the Baltimore Colts and the New York Giants. In that sudden-death overtime gridiron contest, which went down in history as the most exciting and greatest pro football game ever played, Berry helped the Colts win the pro football championship of the world by catching 12 key passes for 178 yards.

In all, Raymond Berry starred for the Baltimore Colts for 13 years, and again and again he led the National Football League in receiving. His matchless pass-catching helped the Colts win the NFL championship again and again — once three times in a row. He became pro football's greatest lifetime pass catcher by setting an all-time record of 631 receptions.

In 1973, when Raymond Berry was in his 40's, he became officially identified as one of the greatest pass-catching marvels pro football ever had. He was enshrined in the Professional Football Hall of Fame as an immortal of the game.

BENNY FRIEDMAN
The Football Flinger

The son of a poor Russian immigrant tailor, Benny Friedman was born and raised in Cleveland, Ohio. Although he was an outstanding all-around high school athlete and a noted local football star, nevertheless, when he entered the University of Michigan in 1923 he had to work at several jobs to earn money for his tuition.

In his sophomore year he tried out for the Michigan football team and made it as a halfback, but spent the first half of his first varsity season sitting on the bench. Because he was 70 inches tall and 170 pounds heavy, his coach didn't think Benny was big enough to play Big-Ten college football. Benny almost quit the football team in frustration.

When he was finally called upon to perform as a substitute quarterback, Friedman quickly revealed himself as a complete football player destined for gridiron glory. He was a brilliant field director, an exceptional passer, a long-distance kicker, a swift-footed runner, and a fine blocker, too. He made Michigan one of the greatest college football teams in history, while he gained national fame as the most spectacular quarterback of his or any time.

"The forward pass is a useful thing
When Benny Friedman makes the fling."

So went a favorite limerick in Benny Friedman's football time in praise of his talent as a passer. He wound up his college years of gridiron glory not only honored as an All-American, but he was among the first to be chosen for enshrinement in the National College Football Hall of Fame.

Benny Friedman was not yet done with gridiron fame, however. In 1927, he entered the pro football ranks to play for the newly organized Cleveland Bulldogs of the National Football League and became an immediate sensation. As a quarterback, he was the first to recognize the potentialities of the forward pass as a touchdown weapon, on a par with the running play.

The advent of Benny Friedman into pro football signalled the start of a new exciting era for the sport. Finesse became more important than brute strength. Before that, a quarterback rarely, if ever, threw a forward pass before the third down. Benny changed all that. He passed *any* time from *any* spot on the field, either on the first or second down. He forced the defense out of its stereotyped strategy and injected thinking into defensive play. Where defenses had consisted of seven-, eight- or nine-men lines in all but the most obvious passing situations, with Benny flinging unexpected forward passes, pro teams began stationing their centers behind the line with instructions to "rove," as middle linebackers do today.

Benny Friedman's most spectacular success in pro football was with the New York Giants. Almost single-handedly he carried the Giants to victory and glory for three seasons. In 1934, at the age of 29, though still one of the highest-paid players in the game, he wearied of pro football, and quit to become a well-known college football coach.

But his greatness as a quarterback will never fade from memory. For when Benny Friedman was in his glory days as a flinger of forward passes, he was the equal of any quarterback immortal who ever performed on a football field.

BOBBY LAYNE
Winning Was Everything

Bobby Layne, who pitched himself into Pro Football's Hall of Fame with fifteen years of brilliant quarterbacking, always said there was little difference in the talent level of pro quarterbacks. He said that winning came about through leadership, by having your men believe in you.

And leadership was a quality Layne had lots of. It made the teams he directed winners — from high school days on. He was a winner in college and three times he led the Detroit Lions to conference championships, on two occasions going on to the world title.

Layne was a Texan, the kind of hero Texans brag about. He was born in 1926 in the small town of Santa Anna, where his father died when Bobby was six years old. He went to live with an aunt and uncle in Fort Worth, and later they moved to Dallas. Bobby's ambition was to be a baseball pitcher and he was good enough to win an athletic scholarship to the University of Texas. In his baseball years there, Layne won twenty-six games, including three no-hitters, and never lost a game.

In football, he was almost as good, leading the Longhorns to twenty-eight victories in the thirty-four games he played for them. He was drafted by the Pittsburgh Steelers, but was traded im-mediately to the Chicago Bears. The Bears thought they didn't need him, either, because Sid Luckman was still playing and his back-up quarterback was Johnny Lujack, the Notre Dame super-star.

So Layne was shunted off to the New York Bulldogs, a poor excuse for a pro football team. Despite Layne's heroic ef-forts, the Bulldogs rarely won. Layne was so disillusioned that he planned to quit the game. But that year, 1951, the Bulldogs traded him to the Detroit Lions. He was there for eight years and became the toast of the Motor City.

In 1952, before Layne was firmly established at the helm, Detroit lost two of its first three games. Then Layne took over as No. 1 quarterback, and the team roared through the rest of the season to establish a 9-3 record and a tie with Los Angeles at the top of the division. In the playoff the Lions beat the Rams, 31-21.

Then, against the mighty Cleveland Browns, who were considered invincible, Layne again led Detroit to victory, a convincing 17-7 triumph which gave the Lions their first championship in seventeen years.

In 1953, Bobby's superb play-calling sparked Detroit to another conference championship with ten victories in twelve games. Again, in the title playoff, the Lions stopped Cleveland in a heartthrobbing 17-16 game. Detroit won its third division title in a row in 1954, but this time in the playoff they ran into a vengeful Cleveland team, which walloped the Lions, 56-10.

Layne suffered a shoulder separation after that season when a horse he was holding suddenly bolted. Layne was used sparingly, but he was hardly the Layne of the championship years. Then, a few years later, when he was thirty-two, Detroit traded him to Pittsburgh.

When he arrived there in 1958, the Steelers already had lost two games, and they lost two of their next three to register a 1-4 record. Layne rallied the team and made the players believe in themselves, so much so that they won five games in a row for a 7-4-1 season record. It wasn't good enough to win, but it was the best the Steelers had done in sixteen years, thanks to the remarkable Texan.

Bobby Layne played through 1962 with Pittsburgh until he was thirty-five, when he hung up his cleats and retired to Lubbock, Texas.

In 1967, Bobby Layne received the honors due one of the greatest of quarterbacks. He was enshrined in the National Professional Hall of Fame as an immortal of the game. He had a most remarkable pro career passing record for his everlasting fame. He had completed 1,814 passes in 3,700 attempts, for 26,721 yards, and 194 touchdowns.

CHARLEY TRIPPI
He Never Tripped on His Run to Fame

Pro football was a simpler game when Charley Trippi arrived on the scene in 1947. The specialists hadn't arrived yet and there was still room for a triple-threat (run-pass-kick) back of Trippi's caliber, and he went out and proved it.

He had been an All-America performer at the University of Georgia and had spent three years with the all-star Third Air Force team in Tampa, Florida. As a rookie with the Chicago (later St. Louis) Cardinals, he turned in a scintillating season in all three of his specialties — running, passing and kicking. The Cardinals rollicked to a nine-victory, three-defeat year and went on to smash the Philadelphia Eagles in the title playoff, thanks in large measure to Charley Trippi.

On an icy field, in frigid weather, the Cardinals went after their first world's title. Trippi squirted through tackle on a quick opener and scooted 44 yards for a touchdown. In the third period, he ran a punt back through the whole Eagle team for 75 yards and another Card touchdown. They were the highlights in a thrilling Chicago victory, with Trippi being credited with 206 yards on fourteen carries and with 102 yards on two punt returns. The final score was 28-21. So began Charley Trippi's eight-year career in big-league pro football.

Trippi was born in Pittston, Pennsyl-
vania, in 1923. As a schoolboy, he weighed less than 160 pounds, but he still wanted to be a tackle. His high school coach switched him to the backfield when he saw how many things the youngster could do.

He had trouble finding a college that

wanted a back as light as he, so he worked his way down the Eastern seaboard until Georgia took him on. He made such an impression on the Bulldog coach that the coach switched his All-America tailback, Frankie Sinkwich, to fullback, to make room for Trippi in the starting lineup. Trippi and Sinkwich took that Georgia team to the Rose Bowl in 1942, with the nineteen-year-old Trippi pacing the team to a 9-0 defeat of UCLA.

Later, Trippi went into the service and was named to the All-Service team as a member of the Third Air Force backfield. When he returned to civilian life to play for Georgia, he led the Bulldogs to an undefeated season, including victories over the tough University of North Carolina (with Choo Choo Justice) and Tulsa in the Oil Bowl. Charley won the Maxwell Award and an All-America rating with his fourteen touchdowns, 744 yards rushing, and 622 yards passing. His punting was as impressive as usual. For his brilliant college playing, he gained membership in the National Collegiate Hall of Fame.

When he turned pro in 1947, he was in the fortunate position of choosing between the New York Yankees of the newly organized All-America Conference and the Chicago Cardinals of the National Football League. He chose the NFL — wisely, as it turned out for that 6-foot, 190-pound halfback, since the AAC went out of existence two years later.

After his sensational rookie season, when he helped the Cardinals become pro football champions of the world, Trippi, who could do it all (run, pass, kick and receive), continued his yeoman work in 1948, sparking the Chicago Cardinals to eleven victories out of twelve games

played. But, unfortunately, on the day of the championship game for the NFL title, ill fortune struck the team against the Philadelphia Eagles. One of the worst snowstorms in that area's history dominated that championship game. The spectacular Charley Trippi found himself trapped in the deep snow pouring down throughout the game, and as a result he was held to a mere 26 yards rushing. That championship game was decided in the final minutes, on a recovered fumble, with the Cardinals losing it by a 7-0 score.

The Cardinals never won another division title after that, but Charley Trippi continued to be an amazing pro performer until 1955. His career came to an end that year, following a severe collision with a rival player. It rendered Charley Trippi unconscious for hours, and he needed plastic surgery for his full recovery. He never played football again, but by that time his fame as one of the truly greats of the big-league pro game was assured.

He had rolled up a host of records in his glorious years starring for the Cards. He had rushed for a total of 3,506 yards with 687 carries. He had caught 130 passes for 1,321 yards, and he had completed 205 of 434 forward passes, for 2,547 yards. Also, he had punted 196 times for an average of almost 50 yards per punt. Moreover, he had returned 63 punts for 864 yards, plus 60 kickoffs for 1,457 yards. He had scored 37 touchdowns. His coach, Jimmy Conzelman, publicly acclaimed him to be the greatest football player he had coached in two decades.

The final honor in tribute to his greatness as a big-league pro player came when Charley Trippi was enshrined in the National Pro Football Hall of Fame, ever to be remembered as one of the immortals of professional football.

STEVE VAN BUREN
The Orphan Boy Who Almost Missed Immortality

In the 1940's, when big-league professional football was mainly dominated by the powerful Philadelphia Eagles, it was said that the invincible Eagle offense could be described by one key play: "Give the ball to halfback Steve Van Buren and let him run!" He was such an overpowering runner that at one time he held six different National Football League records for rushing and scoring.

With awesome Van Buren pulverizing enemy lines (he led the league in rushing in four of his eight years in the majors), the Eagles flew high to glory by winning three consecutive division titles, 1947, 1948, 1949, and turned two of those into world championships — in 1948 and 1949. Each time, Steve Van Buren's blasting his way over all enemy tacklers in quest of yardage was responsible for the Eagles' great triumphs.

Though the Eagles lost to the Chicago Cardinals in the 1947 playoff for football's biggest title (the year Van Buren made history by setting a new NFL rushing record at 1,008 yards), they came back to beat the Cardinals, in 1948, in an historic snow blizzard, for the world's pro football championship. That 7-to-0 victory was produced by a mighty Van Buren

touchdown plunge. It was the first championship ever for the Eagles, and another unforgettable glory-feat for Steve Van Buren.

The following season (1949), which saw halfback Van Buren break his own record rushing mark, he was even more magnificent in the championship playoff game for the NFL title. Though that championship game against the Los Angeles Rams was played in a torrential rain, and in a sea of mud, Van Buren's awesome rushing power was beyond compare. He sloshed through the enemy defenses for a spectacular 196 yards on 31 carries to produce a 14-to-0 victory and once again make the Eagles pro football champions of the world. Steve Van Buren's gridiron exploits made him more than the Eagles' "greatest player" in that club's history. It made him the equal of the greatest rushing halfbacks in all football history.

Surprisingly, Steve Van Buren almost did not become a football player. Born in 1921, in Tele, Honduras, where his father was a fruit inspector, misfortune came early into his life. Both of his parents died when he was very young, and he was sent off to New Orleans to live with his grandparents.

Although he developed an interest in football when he was at Warren Eastern High School, he was nevertheless quickly discouraged from trying out for the football team because he was only a 125-pound stripling. He dropped out of school after his sophomore year and worked in a foundry for two years to build himself up. He returned to high school as a broad-shouldered, muscular 155-pounder, and he played schoolboy football well enough to gain an athletic scholarship to Louisiana State University.

He became a college football halfback brilliant enough to make some headlines and attract the attention of big-league professional football scouts. In 1944, the Philadelphia Eagles acquired him as a pro player for National Football League competition. By that time, Van Buren stood 6-feet-1 inch tall, and was 200 pounds heavy.

As a pro rookie halfback, Van Buren revealed himself as a fierce blocker, a fine punter, and a sure-handed receiver of forward passes, but all he wanted to do for his fame was run through enemy lines of scrimmage. There was nothing fancy nor glamorous about his fearsome rushing. He was sheer raw power in action. He hardly ever tried to dodge enemy tacklers. He loved to run right over them.

In his first season, though felled by influenza and an appendicitis attack, he managed to average 5.5 yards every time he carried the ball. In his second season, he upped that to 5.8 yards per carry, and led the league in both rushing and scoring. He ripped opposing lines to shreds, season after season.

In 1950, however, the most feared rusher in the NFL suffered so many injuries that his magnificent pro career went into a decline. Because of it, the reign of the Philadelphia Eagles as the most powerful team in the league came to an end. They would not win another title for more than a decade.

Van Buren's football career came to an abrupt end early in the 1952 season when he suffered a torn ligament in his left knee. So, after only eight seasons in the pro ranks, he retired as a player. He left behind him a record of 1,320 carries for 5,800 yards, and 69 touchdowns. It was an impressive hunk of glory for the one-time stripling orphan boy who almost never became a football player.

But Steve Van Buren was to enrich his name for posterity with even greater football glory. In 1965, he was enshrined in the Hall of Fame at Canton, Ohio, where now dwell all the immortals of professional football.

VINCE LOMBARDI
Mr. Pro Football

In 1959, Vince Lombardi became a big-time professional head football coach for the first time, assuming command of the Green Bay Packers. The team he inherited was the doormat of the National Football League and was in the depths of despair. The mediocre and futile Packers had won only one game of the twelve scheduled NFL contests they had played in the 1958 football season, and the loyal citizens of the town of Green Bay, many of whom owned bits and pieces of the team, were worried because Green Bay was in danger of losing its football-club franchise to some big city.

Upon Lombardi's arrival, they all hoped that in time he would overhaul and improve the winless Packers and shape them into a respectable pro football team. But no one envisioned the new coach as a miracle worker.

Almost overnight, however, the in-

tense, grim, and little-known Vince Lombardi molded the Green Bay Packers into a contender for football's highest honors and into the football champions of the world, within only three seasons. In the nine years he coached at Green Bay, he built the Packers into a football dynasty.

Under the incomparable coaching genius of Vince Lombardi, the Packers won 89 games in regular National Football League play and scored 141 gridiron victories in all. He masterminded them to six Western Conference titles and five world championships. Lombardi piloted the Green Bay Packers to three National Football League championships in a row, a feat no other coach in professional football history had ever accomplished. Moreover, only he ever coached a team to victory twice in the famed post-season Super Bowl classic. Each time, his Packers crushed the American Football League champions in the battle for the honor of being acclaimed as the greatest team in the whole world of football.

From his humble beginning to his glorious end as the Green Bay Packers' mentor, he was a strange and unqiue pacemaker for gridiron greatness. Although he coached grown men who played football mainly for pay, Coach Lombardi nevertheless treated his players like an old-fashioned despotic father. He drove them hard, and he drilled into all his players his belief in the importance of three things: the family, religion, and the Green Bay Packers. Players who didn't think like Coach Lombardi or play his way did not stay on the Packer team very long. He imposed his will on all his players to gain his winning goals. He commanded matchless respect and obedience. He also demanded of his players

exemplary conduct on and off the football field, as an example to young people.

A man of tireless energy, fiercely devoted to coaching, Lombardi worked seven days a week during the training and playing season and put in fourteen- to sixteen-hour days to produce his unbeatable teams. For each game his team had to play he made warlike preparations. His players were briefed again and again on what he had learned. No rival football coach ever surprised a Lombardi team. His search for perfection in his players was insatiable. He inspired a winning attitude.

"The Packers think and behave like a championship team," the dour, blunt-talking Lombardi often said. "We come to every game to win!"

His players, from the greenest rookie to the most famous star, had boundless faith in him. Even rival coaches came to believe that he could create gridiron miracles beyond the ken of ordinary mortals.

He became famous and feared for doing the unexpected. His team played hard-hitting, powerful, knock-'em-down, solid football.

He established a matchless far-flung scouting system for college football talent. He had an uncanny ability to out-think the opposition in trading and drafting collegiate talent for the big time.

Vince Lombardi came to his exalted position as the most famous and greatest coach in professional football history the hard way. Born in Brooklyn, the son of a poor Italian laborer, he first played football on the sidewalks of New York. A rugged but unspectacular guard for his high-school football team, young Vince won his first grid fame at Fordham University as part of a group. In 1935, he was a tough linesman for a powerful Fordham football team which became famous for its mighty front line known as the "Seven Blocks of Granite."

Upon being graduated from college in 1937, Lombardi went on to law school, but later decided to take a job teaching Latin and physics at St. Cecelia High School in Englewood, New Jersey. While there, he was persuaded to coach the school's football team. Under his coaching, that schoolboy team won thirty-six victories in a row.

His record of success earned for him a call to return to his alma mater to coach the Fordham University freshman football team. But he soon became restless for more important coaching chores, and he became the backfield coach at the United States Military Academy under the famous West Point coach, Colonel Earl ("Red") Blaik. After five years of obscure coaching in college football, Vince Lombardi came to an important turn on the road to gridiron glory. He entered the big-time professional ranks as an offensive backfield coach for the New York Giants of the National Football League. There he remained until he was summoned to Green Bay to become head football coach of the winless Packers and save them from despair and disaster. Thus was a football dynasty born.

For nine years that little packing town in the Midwest was Vince Lombardi's fiefdom, as he became the "Lord and Master" of Green Bay. There he found fame never equaled by any other coach in big-league pro football history. Over the years, although he assembled many outstanding football stars to play for the Packers, he himself was always Green Bay's most celebrated football idol. Throughout the sports world, Coach Lombardi was better known than any of his players. He was paid an enormous salary. So deep was the pride and love the townsfolk had for him that a street which runs past the Packers' home football field was named Lombardi Avenue, in his honor.

At the end of the 1967 football season, although the Green Bay Packers were still the invincible football champions of the world, Coach Lombardi suddenly retired as their football mentor. He was only fifty-four, in the prime of his fabulous career, and still the smartest, the most successful, and the greatest coach in football.

But soon he grew restless in his retirement, and he returned to the pro coaching ranks to accept a new challenge for his fame. He became the coach of an inept and winless Washington Redskins team. Quickly, his coaching genius transformed the Redskins into a winner of the National Football League. Once again, pro football expected a fabulous Lombardi winning saga to be created for history.

A cruel fate intervened, however, in 1970, when coach Vince Lombardi suddenly died, a victim of cancer, at age 57.

He left behind him the glorious legacy of a fantastic pacemaker, with a record of 160 victories achieved in hardly more than a single decade. It was a feat unequaled in pro football history.

"Mr. Pro Football," as Vince Lombardi was known, was as close to being the perfect coach as can be imagined. The game may never know his like again.

BILL DUDLEY
Versatile and Efficient

When Bill Dudley tried out for his high school team in Bluefield, Virginia, he didn't make it because the school didn't have a uniform small enough to fit him. He stood only five-foot-nine and weighed only 150 pounds. Later, they took him on when his weight went up to 156.

Yet, Bill Dudley went on to make his high school team, became an All-America at the University of Virginia, and one of the great pro players of the Forties. He was Number One draft choice of the Pittsburgh Steelers in 1942, and that club, with not-too-impressive personnel, won seven of its last nine games. Dudley was named Rookie of the Year.

It was war time, of course, and the following year he joined the Army Air Corps. In his football play for that branch of the service he was outstanding. He was named an All-Service halfback, and was signed by the Pittsburgh Steelers after the war. He was one of the last of the 60-minute, both-platoon players, a splendid punter and field-goal kicker, besides being a stalwart on defense. And he was such a good open-field runner that one year he was named Most Valuable Player of the National Football League.

Later, he was traded to the Detroit Lions, with whom he played for three seasons, and one day returned a punt 84 yards for a touchdown just after running a kickoff for 78 yards and another score. He established club records in every department on the offense — and continued his brilliant defensive work. Still later, he played for the Washington Redskins.

In 1950, however, when professional football adopted the unlimited-substitution rule, 28-year-old Bill Dudley realized that the day of the football specialist had arrived, and there would be no need for an all-around player of his kind who could block, run, pass and kick with equal efficiency. So he quit the game. But his brilliant nine years as a pro player gained for him a most rewarding honor for his fame. He was elected to the Pro Football Hall of Fame, ever to be remembered as a gridiron immortal.

EARL ("DUTCH") CLARK
The General

One of the charter members of Pro Football's Hall of Fame was Earl Harry ("Dutch") Clark, the quarterback. Though he led his club to only one championship in five years, he was named All-League quarterback in four of those seasons.

In those days, quarterback meant tailback, the man who called the signals, and one of Clark's claims to fame was that he was one of the brainiest signal-callers of all time. Somebody once said, "If Clark stepped on the field with Red Grange, Jim Thorpe and George Gipp, Dutch would be the general."

Clark was born in Fowler, Colorado, in 1906, and grew up in Pueblo. He chose, after a brilliant high school career, to go to Colorado College and was so outstanding that he was chosen as All-Rocky Mountain for three straight years. Then, in 1929, he won national attention for making the All-America team.

From there he went on to the pros and starred with the Portsmouth Spartans, who were to become the Detroit Lions. The Lions lost only three of thirteen games, and one year (1934) recorded a remarkable record of seven consecutive shutouts to open the season. In those seven shutouts, the Lions' opponents never got closer than the Detroit 20-yard line. In 1935, Clark led the Lions to the championship.

Later, he became the Lion coach and, before World War II, directed the Cleveland Rams.

He went into the automobile business in Detroit and again was a success. In 1963, the selection board of the Hall of Fame made him one of the first members, along with Red Grange, Jim Thorpe, Sammy Baugh and Bronko Nagurski. Nobody denied that he deserved the honor.

FRANK LEAHY
A Winner from Winner

Frank Leahy came out of Winner, South Dakota, to become the greatest gridiron pupil of the legendary Notre Dame football coach, Knute Rockne. At Notre Dame, in spite of his fame as a college football player, he was a little-known average-rated tackle. But early in his college career he started snaring every bit of valuable information and gridiron theory offered by his fabulous coach. It was Frank Leahy's ambition to become just as famous a football coach as Rockne.

When he graduated in 1931, he lost no time in becoming a football coaching assistant at several colleges. After eight obscure years of coaching, he became a head football coach at Boston University. In 1941, his alma mater called him, and Frank Leahy eagerly and happily returned to Notre Dame as head football coach. There he remained until 1953, winning national fame as Notre Dame's "second" Knute Rockne. As one of college football's greatest coaches, his winning exploits made him an Irish coaching legend.

He brought the "Fighting Irish" to new heights of gridiron glory, piloting them to six undefeated seasons and four national championships. He became famed throughout the football world as the classic gridiron battler. By the time

he retired at age 45 because of ill health, he had seen 36 of his players win All-American honors, and a host of them star in pro football. In his 13 years as a head football coach, Frank Leahy had piloted his teams to 107 victories and only 13 defeats. Only the immortal Knute Rockne had compiled a higher won-lost percentage among college football coaches in the game's history. Ironically, the amazing Frank Leahy had to wait 17 years before he was enshrined in the National College Football Hall of Fame, ever to be remembered as one of the immortals of the gridiron game.

120

CHARLEY BRICKLEY
The Kicking Marvel

In 1912, when a curly-haired laughing sophomore named Charley Brickley became eligible to play varsity football for Harvard University, there came upon the gridiron stage the most incredible, most spectacular kicking performer ever seen in college football.

He had come to Harvard with a great reputation as a schoolboy athlete, and he enriched it with imperishable glory as a kicking wonder. Charley Brickley was in his time an outstandingly versatile football player. He was an able and speedy ball carrier, a deadly blocker and tackler, and a punter beyond compare. With his educated toe, he made Harvard invincible on the football field. Again and again, he won games for the Crimson with his toe by scores of 3-0.

Often, just before the start of important games, his wily coach, Percy Haughton, would have a hundred footballs placed on the field at various angles and distances, and would order Brickley to boot every one of them through the goal posts. Brickley never missed even one. It always gave opposition players seeing that awesome performance a bad case of pre-game nerves. In every game Harvard played, the Crimson player feared most was punter Charley Brickley. Often he pulled out victories from a near-loss with spectacular drop-kick or placement

field goals. Almost anytime Brickley was inside the 50-yard line, he was good for three points. In his first two varsity seasons, he kicked 34 field goals in 37 attempts. And twice he made Walter Camp's famed All-America team. Charley Brickley never played in a losing game.

His most heroic feat as a kicking

superman was performed on November 22, 1913, when Harvard tangled with its traditional rival, Yale, in a game for both the Ivy League title and for the national college football championship. Early in that game, Brickley came out of a pileup with both eyes so badly scratched that he was nearly blind. But even though he could hardly see, he refused to leave the game, and snapped at his coach: "I don't have to see to kick field goals."

On that unforgettable afternoon, wondrous Charley Brickley kicked five field goals, from distances of 40 to 60 yards, to score all of Harvard's 15 points, winning that game for the Crimson football team and making Harvard the national college football champion.

Charley Brickley is in the National College Football Hall of Fame as one of the immortals of the game. Though he now belongs to faraway football yesterdays, and to a long-gone era of college football, memories of him as the most incredible, most spectacular, and greatest kicker in the history of college football are still vivid.

WILLIE HESTON
One Hundred Touchdowns

The greatest scorer in all college football history was halfback Willie Heston of Michigan University. Twice an All-American (1903-1904), he was the iron man of his era. He ran with amazing speed and crashed through all enemy lines without benefit of interference by his teammates. During Heston's varsity career, Michigan fielded the most powerful college football team ever put together, and halfback Heston always was the spearhead of the attack. He sparked Michigan to 43 victories and one tie in 44 games. In that awesome victory stretch, Michigan rolled up 2,326 points against 38 for the opposition. Willie Heston was that team's human scoring machine. That amazing halfback-great and Hall of Fame immortal scored 100 touchdowns during his fabulous college career. It's an all-time record for the ages.

CLARKE HINKLE
"Block and Tackle"

There never was a more awesome battering-ram fullback in football than Clarke Hinkle.

He came out of Philadelphia to star for Bucknell University. After a dazzling college career, the 200-pound, six-footer "Hink" came to the Green Bay Packers in search of pro football fame and fortune.

He soon established himself as just about the greatest all-around fullback ever to play in the National Football League. He blocked and tackled with frightening power. He punted and place-kicked with the best players of his time. He also was an amazing pass receiver. And when it came to the art of defense against enemy aerial attack, he had no superior in big-league pro football.

Again and again he was named to the All-League team, and three times his fearless and awesome battering-ram playing as a fullback sparked the Packers to a Division crown—and twice to the world pro football championship. During his ten glorious seasons as a superstar of the pro game, he gained 3,860 yards in 1,171 carries.

When he was formally honored as a true immortal of the game—by way of enshrinement in the Professional Football Hall of Fame—everybody who had ever seen mighty fullback Hinkle play said, "They won't ever come any better than Clarke Hinkle!"

ROY ("LINK") LYMAN
The Tackler

One of the great tackles of the early days of pro football was Roy ("Link") Lyman, out of Table Rock, Pawnee County, Nebraska. Even though he did not play high school football (there weren't enough boys), he was outstanding at the University of Nebraska, and in 1921 his team scored 283 points to only 17 for opponents.

A reason for the low point total for Nebraska's foes was Lyman, a ferocious tackle who, even though weighing in at close to 250 pounds, was as agile as a rabbit. He was the first lineman to change positions while a play was in progress, thus confusing the rival backs.

After he was graduated at Nebraska, Lyman signed with the Canton Bulldogs and led them to the National Football League title in his rookie year, 1922. They repeated the following year. Both seasons they were undefeated. Then Link moved on to Cleveland — and it won the championship. He was All-League tackle each of these years.

Then he signed on with the Chicago Bears and was a terror in the Chicago line, playing both offense and defense, from 1926 through 1934. The Bears won the title in 1933 and a division crown in 1934.

Later, Lyman became line coach at his alma mater, the University of Nebraska, and still later, after retiring from football, became owner of an insurance company in San Marino, California.

His memories included sixteen seasons of football—college, semi-pro and pro—and only one of his teams had a losing year. Naturally, he wound up immortalized in Pro Football's Hall of Fame, for his everlasting glory as an all-time tackle.

EARL ("CURLY") LAMBEAU
Personification of the Packers

He was born in Green Bay, Wisconsin, on April 9, 1898, son of a building contractor, and Earl Louis ("Curly") Lambeau, before he was twenty years old, practically single-handedly put Green Bay on the football map.

Curly attended East High School, which had been beaten for seven consecutive years by its traditional rival, West High. Lambeau turned that around and with spectacular passing exhibitions trounced East High's most important foe. That was only the first of Curly's exciting triumphs.

In 1918, he enrolled at Notre Dame, where there was a new coach named Knute Rockne. Lambeau played halfback and fullback for the Rock, and though only a freshman, became one of the thirteen lettermen that year.

After the season, he went home to undergo a tonsillectomy and decided not to return to South Bend. Instead, he went to work for Frank Peck, who owned the Indian Packing Company, and formed the Green Bay Packers. They became part of the American Professional Football Association and later the new National Football League.

Using a flashy passing attack, the Packers became one of the finest teams in the pro game. By 1927, the club finished second in the twelve-club league, and in 1929, it went undefeated, rack-

ing up twelve victories and a tie. The Packers won the title again in 1930, and again in 1931, something no other team had done before. Lambeau played through the 1931 season.

Lambeau was an exceptionally able scout and picked off some astounding players, including the exceptional Don Hutson. Later, Lambeau left Green Bay to coach the Chicago Cardinals and the Washington Redskins.

But when he died in 1965, everybody said the same thing: "Curly Lambeau *was* the Green Bay Packers!" He was also a gridiron immortal, enshrined in the Pro Football Hall of Fame for imperishable glory.

GEORGE McAFEE
Running Wild

For a pro football halfback, George McAfee was a puny one at 165 pounds, yet he became one of the finest open-field runners of all time.

He came out of Duke University to play for the Chicago Bears of the National Football League, and he was a brilliant star from the beginning. He returned enemy punts for eighty and ninety yards. In his rookie season, he was a vital player of that awesome Chicago team which made history by crushing the powerful Washington Redskins by an unbelievable score of 73-0, for the NFL championship. The next year (1941), Speedy McAfee again helped the Bears win the pro football championship of the world. Then, until 1946, he went into military service. When he returned to the Chicago Bears, they again won the National Football League title.

Despite his tiny size, McAfee performed astonishing feats as a major-league pro football player. Though he played in pro football's "one-platoon era," he did much more than just gallop with the ball for sensational long runs. He was an outstanding defensive player and an excellent punter. He once booted a 79-yard kick — the longest ever achieved by a Chicago Bear .player. Once, he set an incredible league record by averaging 12.8 yards on 112 punt returns. Rival coaches used to tell their kickers, "Punt to anybody but McAfee."

Indeed, little George McAfee was something special as a gridiron great. And great was his reward as a ball-carrier. He was enshrined in Pro Football's Hall of Fame with all the other immortals of the game.

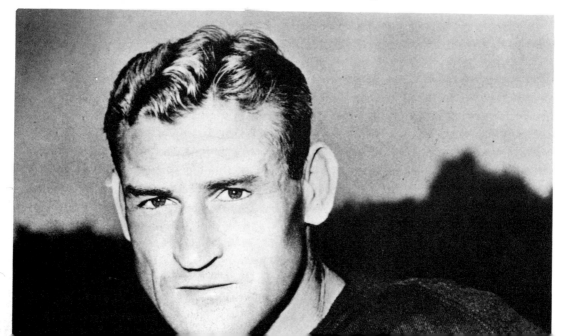

GUY CHAMBERLIN
"He Never Learned How to Lose"

Guy Chamberlin, who was named to Pro Football's Hall of Fame in 1965, came off a Nebraska farm to become one of the great players and great coaches of the game.

At the University of Nebraska before World War I (Chamberlin was born in 1894) he was an All-America halfback with "the finest stiff-arm the game had ever seen." He struck fear in the hearts of most defensive players and was the most talked-about back in the Midwest.

Chamberlin went into the Army after that and then played for Jim Thorpe's Canton Bulldogs. He also played for George Halas's Decatur Staleys, the team that was to become the Chicago Bears. The team won 21 games, lost two, and tied two during his time. The following year he returned to Canton as player-coach and the Bulldogs did not lose a single game in two years.

That team first moved to Cleveland and then to Frankford, a Philadelphia suburb, where the renowned Yellow-jackets won the National Football League title in a thrilling game against the Bears. Chamberlin served not only as coach, but also as the game-saving end. He blocked Paddy Driscoll's field-goal attempt in the closing minutes, and Frankford won, 7-6.

During the Hall of Fame ceremonies in 1965, Red Blaik, Army's celebrated coach, said, "Chamberlin never learned how to lose."

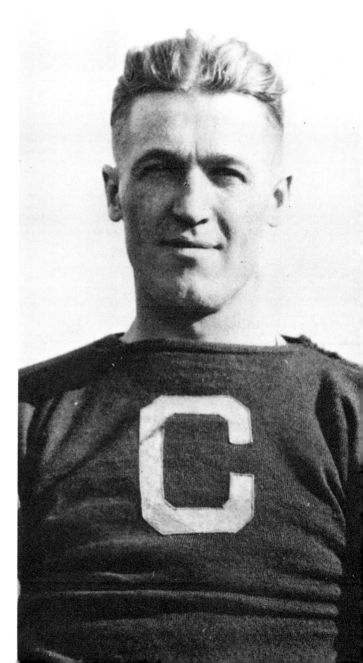

DANNY FORTMANN
The Medic

In the early days of professional football, nobody ever heard of salaries such as half a million dollars a year. Danny Fortmann, who played for the Chicago Bears in the late Thirties and early Forties, never made more than $6,000 a year — and that was his high, after having broken in at $1,700 as a rookie in 1936.

Yet he was a tremendous performer, as guard for the Bears for eight years, during which time his club won four division titles. On offense (they played two ways in those days), Fortmann called signals for the linemen and was a slugging blocker. On defense, he was a deadly tackler, though he weighed less than 200 pounds.

He was only nineteen years old when he came up, the youngest starting player in the league. Fortmann had been to Colgate University, and he had ambition to be a doctor. (He applied to the University of Chicago Medical School and he was the last one accepted that year. The dean had eliminated all applicants but two, so he said to his secretary, "Which one? Both are Phi Beta Kappas. One is a football player, the other is a violin player." The secretary happened to be a football fan.)

Danny Fortmann, who played pro football to earn the money he needed to pay for his medical education, became a noted physician. But he also became a noted guard in football history. He is one of the immortals in Pro Football's Hall of Fame.

CLYDE TURNER
The Cowboy Once Known as "Bulldog"

A name that threw terror into the hearts of National Football League backs for a dozen years was that of Clyde ("Bulldog") Turner, the Chicago Bears' ferocious center, who was named to the All-Pro team for eight glorious years in a row. He was a mainstay of the Chicago attack and defense which won five division titles and four world championships in seven years.

There never were any doubts that the Bulldog would be installed in the Professional Football Hall of Fame, which came in 1966, fourteen years after Turner had quit playing.

As a 155-pound high-school player in Sweetwater, Texas, Turner couldn't seem to find his niche. No college was interested in giving him a scholarship in those depression days (1935), so he tried his hand at trading cattle in order to earn enough money to enter college. He chose Hardin-Simmons University in Abilene, and he reported for football practice at a substantial 190 pounds. He was a real Texas cowboy in search of football fame. He became the university's center, even though he had his eye on being a back. But he was to say later that once he started playing center, in those days of one-platoon teams, he knew he had found his place.

After a stickout performance in the East-West Shrine game in San Francisco,

Turner was drafted by the Bears, even though he was still hardly considered a plum of a prospect. ("Who's he?" asked one owner. "And what is Hardin-Simmons?") Though the Detroit Lions made some half-hearted passes at him, Clyde signed with the Bears.

He joined one of the strongest teams of the era, the team which routed the Washington Redskins in the title game, 73-0, with rookie Turner doing his bit — intercepting a pass in the third period and racing twenty-four yards for a touchdown.

From then on, Bulldog Turner was the most talked-about lineman in the league as the Bears rolled on to victory after victory. Turner's contribution to the well-balanced Chicago performances was

his ability to pull down opposing backs, his amazing blocking, and the way he could intercept opposition passes. In 1942, he led the league in interceptions, even though he had a broken nose most of the year.

Turner quit as a player in 1952, catching on with the Bears as assistant coach. Then, years later, he came back to coach

the ill-fated New York Titans, a club which folded at the end of the season. Bulldog returned to his Texas ranch and his quarter horses.

He also had his memories, though, of the time he was the outstanding lineman of the game for a decade, firmly established in history as professional football's "Mr. Center."

WALT KIESLING
"Big Kies"

Walt Kiesling once was a schoolboy player at Cretin High School in St. Paul, Minnesota. He wasn't too bad, though the school had no gym or locker room, and if you wanted to play, you had to live near enough to the school to go home and get your uniform.

Kiesling later went to St. Thomas College in St. Paul, where the facilities were better. Then, in 1926, he joined Ernie Nevers's Duluth Eskimos, and later the Pottsville Maroons, and still later the Pittsburgh Steelers. He was a splendid guard who was named to the Hall of Fame.

When "Big Kies," as they called him, was joined on the Steelers by Bobby Layne, the Texas quarterback, Layne asked him how long he had played pro ball (1926-1938). Kiesling said, "Until they wouldn't let me suit up any more."

He weighed 265 pounds, and perhaps his best years were when he played for

the Chicago Cardinals from 1929 to 1933. He was the annual All-League selection at guard, even though his club usually wound up in the cellar.

He was coach of the Steelers on four different occasions, certainly a novel course of events, but his failing health made him resign in 1957. He died in 1962, four years before the Hall of Fame elected him to posterity.

PAUL BROWN
Always a Winner

Paul Brown was the only football coach ever to have a team named after him — and he holds the distinction of being such a gridiron genius that he destroyed an entire league.

Brown was named coach and general manager of the Cleveland club of the new All-America Conference, starting in 1946, and the owner had such faith in him that he named the team the Browns. For more than a decade, Cleveland was a football dynasty. Paul Brown became the most dominating figure in the game — and his teams won so often and so convincingly that the AAC faded into oblivion after Cleveland had won 52 games, lost only four, tied two, and had taken the league championship in the four years of the league's existence.

The year after the All-America Conference folded, Paul Brown's Browns joined the National Football League. In their first season (1950), the Browns tied with the New York Giants at the top of the American Conference. Then they defeated the Giants in a playoff and went on to nip the tough Los Angeles Rams for the league title. Cleveland went on to win six division titles and two world championships in the next seven years.

Brown came to the pros with a remarkable record behind him. He was born in Norwalk, Ohio, but his family moved to Massillon when he was twelve. He played football at Massillon High, even though he weighed only 125 pounds, and later was quarterback at a small university in Oxford, Ohio — Miami U.

In 1932, at 24 years of age, he became coach of the Massillon High School team, which he led to six consecutive state titles. One year his team scored 477 points, while giving up only six points to the opposing high schools.

Later, he went to Ohio State and led the Buckeyes to a 6-1-1 record in his first season, followed by a 9-1-0 record the following year. Ohio State was voted the country's No. 1 team. Then in 1944 Brown joined the Navy and took over the football club at the Great Lakes Training Center. He made that team a winner, too, including one spectacular victory over Notre Dame.

While at Great Lakes, he was signed to coach the Cleveland Browns in the new league which was to come into being after World War II. Paul Brown whipped up a team that was to be the scourge of the new league. The Browns virtually eliminated competition and AAC attendance dipped, thus sounding the death knell of the conference.

Then, moving to the National Football League, Brown again was devastating, winning their conference title every year from 1950 through 1955, and capturing the world championship in 1950, 1954 and 1955.

And still Paul Brown wasn't finished. He left Cleveland in 1963 and shifted to the American Football League, where he became coach and general manager of the Cincinnati Bengals. He began building from scratch, just as he had in high school, college, the Navy, and the other pro leagues.

It is no wonder that he was ushered into the professional Hall of Fame with fanfare.

CLIFF BATTLES
The Underpaid Wonder

Cliff Battles, the hard-running halfback of the Boston and Washington teams of the National Football League, was the first man in the history of the league to lead in rushing two years in a row.

He stood only six-feet-one and weighed 195 pounds, yet he outdistanced backs who weighed 50 or more pounds more. In his six short years in professional football, he was named to the All-League team three times. He was able to churn through the line with the power of a fullback, yet he had extraordinary nimbleness as an open-field runner.

Born in Ohio, Battles attended West Virginia Wesleyan College at Buckhannon, where he won letters in basketball, baseball, tennis, and track, in addition to football. He was graduated at the top of his class, was named Phi Beta Kappa, and it's likely he would have become a Rhodes scholar, had he not chosen to play professional football.

At the time, 1931, George Preston Marshall had acquired a new NFL franchise in Boston — the Redskins — and needed talent. His eye was caught by the exploits of young Battles, who though playing on a losing West Virginia Wesleyan team, turned in three magnificent seasons. Marshall sent his business manager to negotiate with Battles and added, "Sign him — or just keep going south."

In his rookie year, Battles did not play much, but in 1933 he became an outstanding rusher, not only winning the title for most yardage gained, but also being named to the All-Pro team.

By 1936, with Battles doing yeoman duty, Boston won the Eastern Dvision championship by defeating the New York Gaints, 14-0, on a muddy field. Battles scored one of the touchdowns on an 80-yard run. In the championship game against the Green Bay Packers that year, Battles was injured in the first period and had to be carried from the field. As a result, Boston lost, 21-6.

The following year, though, when the Redskin franchise was moved from Boston to Washington, Battles' team won the world championship as he rushed for 874 yards and became the first man to repeat as rushing leader.

In winning the Eastern title against the Giants, Battles was superb, ripping holes in the New York line as the Redskins raced to a 49-14 rout. Against the Chicago Bears in the title game, Battles made one touchdown and set up two others as the Redskins ground out a 28-21 victory.

That turned out to be Battles' last game. He had played six years in the pros for $3,000 a year, but when he asked for a raise for the 1938 season, the Redskins turned him down, even though he was the proven best runner in football. So Battles left the pros to become Lou Little's assistant at Columbia University in New York.

In 1955, Battles was named to the Hall of Fame for collegiate immortals, the first player from a small college to be so honored.

Soon after, another honor was bestowed upon him in tribute to his greatness as the best running back of his time in big-league pro football. He was enshrined in the Professional Football Hall of Fame as one of the immortals of the pro game.

RICHARD MARVIN BUTKUS
"The Animal"

Born and raised in Chicago, Illinois, one of nine children in a poor Lithuanian family, Dick Butkus was only an eighth-grade schoolboy when he decided what he would be when he grew up — a professional football player. Husky and tough, he became so outstanding a high-school football star that he earned an athletic scholarship to the University of Illinois.

No sooner had he begun intercollegiate football than he proved himself to be an amazing linebacker. He had the dedication and the heft, as well as a sure instinct to do the right thing at the right time, and garnered many honors for his magnificent defensive playing. In his varsity season he was named the nation's college football player of the year and an All-American for the second time.

In 1965, at the age of 23, Dick Butkus realized his boyhood dream: he became a professional football player. The Chicago Bears lured him into the National Football League with a contract for $235,000. Quickly, the 6-foot-3-inch, 245-pound Butkus proved himself a matchless middle linebacker of tremendous power and awesome strength. He was acclaimed as the rookie of that football year; he also was chosen for the All-NFL football team, along with the best qualified players in the pro game.

As the football seasons passed, Butkus displayed such fierceness and savagery that he was nicknamed "The Animal." He hurt the opposition in every game. Always at the point of attack, he closed off so many holes, knocked down so many enemy passes, and eliminated so many rival players with his destructive tackling, that he became known and feared as a terror who could win a game all by himself. Ranging far afield, always playing defensive football without asking or giving any quarter, mighty Butkus averaged more than 200 tackles each season, more than 25 interceptions, and as many fumble recoveries.

At the age of 31, as a nine-season veteran of big-league pro football, he was still enriching his fame as the greatest middle linebacker of the game in 1973. Fiercely dedicated, he was still a rare superstar, still playing for the Chicago Bears, for an annual salary of $100,000.

He was well on the way to gridiron immortality, already a legendary middle linebacker, acclaimed as the greatest of his time and perhaps of all time.

GEORGE TRAFTON
Top Center

George Trafton played for the Chicago Bears for ten seasons, but he was around even before that — when the Bears were still the Staleys, first in Decatur, Illinois, and then in Chicago.

He was a big, tough center, who, of course, played sixty minutes of every game, and for years he was ranked as the top man at his position.

He was a Chicago boy originally, having played for the Oak Park High School. He enlisted in the Army in 1918. He captained the Camp Grant team and he was sought after by many colleges. He chose Notre Dame, but when he was caught playing semi-pro ball by Knute Rockne, he was expelled.

Then came his days in the pros, with the ferocious Trafton dizzying ball carriers. Later, he became an assistant to Curly Lambeau at Green Bay, and still later he became a professional prize fighter. He once went against Primo Carnera, then being groomed for the heavyweight title, but lasted only fifty-four seconds.

His coaching career lasted only a few years (Green Bay and Cleveland), but when they mention outstanding centers who did their stuff in the pros, George Trafton's name is always up there near the top. His greatness as a center gained for him the most coveted of all gridiron

honors — enshrinement in the Professional Football Hall of Fame as one of the immortals of the game.

JOHN WILLIAM HEISMAN
The Legend of a Trophy

At the conclusion of every intercollegiate football season the outstanding college football player in America is awarded the Heisman Memorial Trophy, bestowed by a vote of the leading historians of the game. It is college football's most coveted and highly prized individual award. Great is the national fame of a "Heisman Winner" as a football hero, and all fans deservedly hail the record of his outstanding gridiron feats.

The odd thing about the Heisman Trophy is that not many people in the football world know anything about the man for whom this famed award is named, despite the fact that few men had as great an impact on the game as John William Heisman, a football coach who ranks with the greatest of all time.

Born in Cleveland, Ohio, in 1869, Heisman played his collegiate football in two places, Pennsylvania University and Brown. At neither college was he more than an average player. He began a coaching career at Oberlin in 1892, and surprisingly remained a college football coach for the next 37 years. Heisman coached football teams at seven different colleges, but wherever he went, he never failed to produce winning teams, some of them the greatest in history.

Starting in 1916, his Georgia Tech national championship team went unbeaten for three seasons in a row. The most memorable win during that long victorious streak was a runaway triumph over Cumberland College by an unbelievable score of 220 to 0! It was the highest score ever achieved by a college football team in a single game, a feat that doubtless will never be equaled.

There never was a more ingenious nor stranger college football coach than John Heisman. His gridiron innovations were numerous and valuable for the growth of football in America.

As legend has it, John Heisman was the real "Father of the Forward Pass." He was the inventor of such football subtleties as the spin play, the direct snap of the ball from center to back, and the hidden-ball trick. His inventive genius devised a system of moving players to produce surprise attacks for scoring touchdowns. It was dubbed the Heisman Shift. He invented the public scoreboard which displayed downs, yards to go, and other important data for fans to know while watching a gridiron contest.

Though acknowledged as one of the greatest of college football coaches, he was an unbelievable eccentric. At his training tables coach Heisman banned hot water and soup for his players, simply because he believed that hot liquids weakened muscles. He also did not allow his players to eat any foods he did not like to eat. Nuts, apples, and coffee were forbidden. Because he liked raw meat, his players were persuaded to eat lots of it.

As one of the most demanding and dictatorial college football coaches ever, he was severe with his players, and expected unquestioned instant obedience to all orders.

Curiously, when John Heisman wasn't busy coaching college football teams, he was winning applause for himself on the legitimate stage as an eminent Shakespearean actor.

Ironically, a meaningless football game cost the life of this fabulous coach. It was perhaps fitting that John Heisman would meet death in unusual fashion. On the afternoon of October 3, 1936, he was watching a football game being played in a cow pasture by a group of neighborhood youngsters. To see that game, Heisman climbed up to a high perch in a tree, fell, and was killed.

Upon John Heisman's departure from this world, the Heisman Memorial Trophy came into being. Today, as it has been now for many years, no greater honor can be bestowed upon a college football player in recognition of his gridiron prowess than to dub him a Heisman Trophy Winner.

The Heisman Memorial Trophy Winners

*(The John Heisman Memorial Trophy is Awarded Annually
to the Nation's Leading College Football Player)*

YEAR	PLAYER	COLLEGE
1935	Jay Berwanger	Chicago
1936	Larry Kelley	Yale
1937	Clint Frank	Yale
1938	Davey O'Brien	Texas Christian
1939	Nile Kinnick	Iowa
1940	Tom Harmon	Michigan
1941	Bruce Smith	Minnesota
1942	Frank Sinkwich	Georgia
1943	Angelo Bertelli	Notre Dame
1944	Les Horvath	Ohio State
1945	Felix Blanchard	West Point (Army)
1946	Glenn Davis	West Point (Army)
1947	John Lujack	Notre Dame
1948	Doak Walker	Southern Methodist
1949	Leon Hart	Notre Dame
1950	Vic Janowicz	Ohio State
1951	Dick Kazmaier	Princeton
1952	Billy Vessels	Oklahoma
1953	John Lattner	Notre Dame
1954	Alan Ameche	Wisconsin
1955	Howard Cassady	Ohio State
1956	Paul Hornung	Notre Dame
1957	John Crow	Texas A&M
1958	Pete Dawkins	West Point (Army)
1959	Billy Cannon	Louisiana State
1960	Joe Bellino	Annapolis (Navy)
1961	Ernie Davis	Syracuse
1962	Terry Baker	Oregon State
1963	Roger Staubach	Annapolis (Navy)
1964	John Huarte	Notre Dame
1965	Mike Garrett	Southern California
1966	Steve Spurrier	Florida
1967	Gary Beban	UCLA
1968	O. J. Simpson	University of Southern California (USC)
1969	Steven Owens	Oklahoma
1970	Jim Plunkett	Stanford
1971	Pat Sullivan	Auburn
1972	John Rodgers	Nebraska

The 10 All-Time Winningest College Football Coaches

	Won	Lost
Amos Alonzo Stagg	314	181
Glenn ("Pop") Warner	313	108
Paul Bryant	220	69
Gilmour Dobie	210	25
Fielding ("Hurry-Up") Yost	196	36
Howard Jones	194	64
Robert Neyland	173	31
Bud Wilkinson	145	29
Jock Sutherland	144	28
H. L. Williams	143	34

The 10 All-Time Winningest Professional Football Coaches

	Coaching Years	Won
George Halas	40	320
Earl ("Curly") Lambeau	33	231
Steve Owen	23	151
Paul Brown	18	138
Weeb Ewbank	19	126
Sid Gillman	16	114
Hank Stramm	13	112
Don Schula	10	105
Buddy Parker	15	102
Tom Landry	13	98